W9-AHG-985

Business-Dō

Business-Dō

THE WAY TO SUCCESSFUL LEADERSHIP

HIROSHI "MICKEY" MIKITANI
Founder & CEO of Rakuten, Inc.

WILEY

Copyright © 2018 by Hiroshi Mikitani. All rights reserved.

Published by John Wiley & Sons, Inc., Hoboken, New Jersey.

Published simultaneously in Canada.

No part of this publication may be reproduced, stored in a retrieval system, or transmitted in any form or by any means, electronic, mechanical, photocopying, recording, scanning, or otherwise, except as permitted under Section 107 or 108 of the 1976 United States Copyright Act, without either the prior written permission of the Publisher, or authorization through payment of the appropriate per-copy fee to the Copyright Clearance Center, Inc., 222 Rosewood Drive, Danvers, MA 01923, (978) 750-8400, fax (978) 646-8600, or on the Web at www.copyright.com. Requests to the Publisher for permission should be addressed to the Permissions Department, John Wiley & Sons, Inc., 111 River Street, Hoboken, NJ 07030, (201) 748-6011, fax (201) 748-6008, or online at www.wiley.com/go/permissions.

Limit of Liability/Disclaimer of Warranty: While the publisher and author have used their best efforts in preparing this book, they make no representations or warranties with respect to the accuracy or completeness of the contents of this book and specifically disclaim any implied warranties of merchantability or fitness for a particular purpose. No warranty may be created or extended by sales representatives or written sales materials. The advice and strategies contained herein may not be suitable for your situation. You should consult with a professional where appropriate. Neither the publisher nor author shall be liable for any loss of profit or any other commercial damages, including but not limited to special, incidental, consequential, or other damages.

For general information on our other products and services or for technical support, please contact our Customer Care Department within the United States at (800) 762-2974, outside the United States at (317) 572-3993, or fax (317) 572-4002.

Wiley publishes in a variety of print and electronic formats and by print-on-demand. Some material included with standard print versions of this book may not be included in e-books or in print-on-demand. If this book refers to media such as a CD or DVD that is not included in the version you purchased, you may download this material at http://booksupport.wiley.com. For more information about Wiley products, visit www.wiley.com.

Library of Congress Cataloging-in-Publication Data is Available:

ISBN 9781119412229 (Hardcover)
ISBN 9781119412212 (ePDF)
ISBN 9781119412250 (ePub)

Cover Image: Mika Ninagawa
Cover Design: Rakuten

Printed in the United States of America.

10 9 8 7 6 5 4 3 2 1

This book is for my partner in life and work and our children.

Contents

Introduction

Dreams are for the young. This is a beautiful saying. But it's wrong. Dreams are the very fuel that moves our society forward.

Although there's nothing wrong with having dreams when you're young, the saying implies that you no longer have time to dream once you grow up and are thrown into the cold reality of society.

I would argue that dreams are even more valuable as you move through your life. But as you leave childhood behind, you must do more than dream. Just having a dream is meaningless. You must turn your dreams into specific goals, work out the steps necessary to achieve them, and then, one by one, actually take those steps. You have to use everything you have—your talents, abilities, strength, and perseverance—to reach these goals.

You need skills to realize your dreams. What's more, you need a system and a process to acquire those skills and execute them. This is what in Japanese we call creating *shikumi*—or systemization. When you pair a dream with a *shikumi,* you may reach even the most extraordinary goals.

I had a dream over two decades ago, and I have spent my whole life since pursuing that dream. The number of people who have joined me in pursuing the same dream has also grown. The company I started with one other person has grown into a company of thousands. And the whole time, I've been constantly asking myself: How can I best communicate my method of achieving dreams and goals? What do you have to do to be truly successful? And what shouldn't you do?

I've put my ideas into words and shared them with my colleagues many times, and I believe Rakuten is what it is today as a result of this effort. The company's continued growth, even through times of global economic crisis, is proof of that.

I share my methods more widely now because we are in an era of great change—a turbulent time when dreams and their execution could not be more important.

We are at a time when it's clear that the internet is not simply a new format—another channel for our existing products and services. Instead, it is a platform on which transformed industries will grow and change. The internet has already reconfigured commerce and the media. It's now far into its transformation of financial services, turning money from bills and coins into a digitized promise and giving rise to a new industry (fintech). It's clear that this is only the start of change that will move through all industries. What will the next new major industry transformations be? Autotech? Pharmatech? Edutech? And as those industries rise up, what new questions will they raise? As the internet becomes the platform for education, of course we rethink the nature of "books" but we can also ask: What is a teacher? What is a classroom? What is a student? How does the internet transform these basic concepts? This is true for every industry. We are also seeing the changes take place in transportation. Already we have AI drones and cars. What is next? Even my own job will face change. Will we see the AI CEO? That's not so farfetched.

In a time of great change, it becomes that much more important to have guiding principles. These are not rules that cut us off from change, but truths that help us navigate it. They are methods that help us move forward and achieve our dreams. They are principles that give us a system in which to operate effectively.

This book, *Business-Dō*, is a detailed look at my guiding principles, offering specific instructions, stories, and techniques to help anyone realize dreams and achieve lasting success. In Japanese characters, "Dō" represents the "way" or the "path" and it can be used to represent an essential philosophy, spirit or a moral code. You might be more familiar with the term "Bushido" which also uses this character and is loosely translated as the way of the warrior. This book breaks down my fundamental philosophy for business and leadership into useful lessons. You can be successful in business as well if you put these lessons into practice. They reflect how I think and act when facing the problems that arise in business. You don't have to learn all the rules. If you follow the ones that speak to you, I'm sure the doors of opportunity will open to you.

Don't be troubled by critics who say dreams and reality are two different things. That's just a spiteful excuse used by those who didn't work hard enough to realize their dreams. Of course dreams and reality are different. But that's why turning dreams into reality is so worthwhile and rewarding—not just for the dreamer, but for all of us who benefit when big dreams become successful reality.

It is my hope that this book helps you realize your dreams. Here's how it's done.

Hiroshi "Mickey" Mikitani

0

Clean Your Space

Why do I have a Chapter 0?

I was through the first draft of this book when I realized I would need a Chapter 0—and that it would be about our ritual at Rakuten of cleaning our workspaces.

There is quite a bit of good advice in this book. But if you only take away one idea, I hope it will be this one: Make sure you clean your office by yourself.

I don't mean set a time for the janitorial staff to come by. That's a different issue. I mean: clean your own workspace. It is a ritual that I believe is a crucial building block of professional success. Sometimes, it is the most basic of rituals that allows us to achieve greatness.

Every week, at the same time in the morning, everyone at Rakuten cleans his or her workspace. We take out the rags and spray bottles. We clean off our surfaces. We pick up any trash. We get down on our hands and knees and polish the legs of our office chairs.

When I say everyone, I mean everyone. You will find me doing this chore every week, without fail.

Why?

It is a question I am asked often, since it's not common for everyone in a company to engage in this behavior. We do it because I know it's important. In fact, I know it's critical to our success.

Like many company rituals, this one started in the earliest days of our company. That's when Rakuten was just a handful of people in a single room, trying to start something big. Every week we cleaned our humble space. We had to. Who else would if we did not?

As we grew, we continued to engage in this ritual—not because we had to, but because we came to understand what it meant. I recognize this is not how many other leaders in Silicon Valley behave. Still, even though it is different from other companies, I know it is something that is very important to me personally, and to the way I want to lead.

For me, personally, cleaning reminds me to be appreciative for what I have. I often find myself thinking about the people who have supported me in my efforts to build this company. I remind myself, in this one moment a week, that I am lucky and that I should remember what got me here.

This is a mindset I spread in Rakuten by making this not just my ritual, but also our ritual. I want us all to take that moment to step back, to be humble, to engage in this shared practice.

A shared practice reminds us that we are all connected. Every job in your company is your job. It's all about whether you fully realize this or not. Those who do not realize this will absolutely never succeed in business. We clean to remind ourselves and each other that there is no job in the company that is unrelated to our own work. We are united, in this one practice and in all the things we do every day. This is a concept that we may remind ourselves of weekly, so that when we face a challenge, we can pull together, draw on that knowledge of connection, and fight as one.

What is more, cleaning reminds us to care. Think about your home for a moment. If you walked into your living room, for example, and you saw a piece of trash on the floor, would you walk around it? Would you ignore it because it was someone else's job to pick it up? Of course not. This is your home, you feel a sense of pride about it. It has a place in your heart. So of course you take the time to take care of it. Your home is worth that one moment it takes to bend down and pick up a piece of trash on the floor. Whenever I am considering investing in a company, I will always look to see how clean the office is. If I go in and it is messy and there is trash on the floor that makes me wonder if the people in the company care about it. A clean office, on the other hand, inspires me to feel confident that this company is united in the pursuit of excellence.

This is the feeling we want to instill here at Rakuten. Many companies may come and go in this world, but only some will achieve greatness. Only a few will change the world. To do this, I believe we must feel about our company the way we feel about our homes. We must feel that sense of pride and be willing to care for it. The company must have a special place in our hearts.

At Rakuten, I look for ways all the time to build that feeling in all of us. The weekly office cleaning is one ritual in which I pursue that goal. We are not just cleaning up our desks in those few minutes. We are engaging in a ritual that reminds us this is a special place. We are here not just to get through the day and make money, but also to do something extraordinary. We care about what we do and we show this in ways that are big—in innovation—and in ways that are small, such as this moment we set aside to take care of the space around us.

Many companies have achieved greatness by incorporating rituals. Sam Walton, founder of Walmart, used to lead store employees in a rousing "Walmart cheer." Many companies hold monthly birthday parties or organize regular volunteer outings. There was once a businessman in Japan who was known, even as his company grew, to go outside each morning and sweep the doorstep of the company entrance. These are rituals and they are all designed to remind the people within a company that they are engaged in something special. They can and should take the time to value that opportunity.

So I place this piece of advice in Chapter 0—a space that is empty and with no distractions. Cleaning your workspace is a simple, easy way to remind yourself that you value the work you are doing. It sets the stage, both physically and mentally, for you to achieve something great. Value the space you are in. Take the moment, put it on your calendar, make it a ritual. Do this and I am sure you will be successful.

1

The 10 Core Principles

The ten business rules explored in this chapter are the foundation of my business philosophy. They are the keys to success, and I review them here in order of importance. I urge you to read these rules in sequence, from the beginning.

01 All concepts are relative

Never believe in the absolute.

No one way of thinking is perfect. Nothing in this world is absolute. Say you turn on a light bulb in a dark room. It feels bright. But step inside a room lit by a single bulb after being outside in the midday sun, and it will seem dark. Everything is relative.

Nothing in human thought is absolutely right. So you shouldn't put your faith in dubious expressions such as, "It's just common sense."

This is my basic philosophy. In fact, common sense itself is often completely arbitrary.

Here's an example: Some 20 years ago, I began my business—an online shopping marketplace. I was not the first to try this. Several other companies including famous leaders such as IBM had tried this, and failed. Because they had failed, many told me I was foolish to try it myself. Online shopping malls won't work, they told me. It's just common sense.

Obviously, that turned out not to be true. It was not "common sense" that blocked online marketplaces from thriving. Online marketplaces were a good idea, waiting for good execution to attract customers. When the right online marketplaces were launched, customers flocked to them. So much for the "common sense" that said it would never work.

Business books repeat *ad nauseam* that you shouldn't fall into the trap of common sense. So why do people continue to do so? We need to seriously consider the reasons for this.

All ways of thinking have strengths and weaknesses. That's why—despite many thousands of years having passed since people started to form societies—humankind still hasn't discovered how to organize a perfect society. Perhaps it never will.

Philosophies, ideas, and ideologies continually evolve and change with surprising fluidity. This is the nature of human society. Nothing is certain. It doesn't follow, however, that nothing has any value.

What's important is to keep moving forward, even if you're unsteady. Children who have just started to walk fall over all the time. You *have* to lose your balance in order to walk. The very act of taking a step forward means being off balance. You lose your balance, then regain it. Repeat this action, and you move forward.

Civilizations and societies seem to progress in essentially the same way. This loss of balance is at the heart of evolution.

I'm not talking in the abstract. Awareness of this idea plays a vital role in all aspects of daily life. And naturally, that includes business.

Don't be afraid of losing your balance and falling over. After all, children learn how to walk by falling. After only six months of practice, they'll rarely stumble.

There's no such thing as a way of thinking that's correct all of the time. That's ultimately why I think "common sense" should be viewed skeptically. Ideas evolve and can be refined when they are thrown off balance.

Be suspicious of common sense. Don't be afraid of defying it. Follow the path you believe in.

02 Believe in the power of the moonshot

Aim high—higher than you think is possible.

Both individuals and businesses have to experience breakthroughs to grow significantly. NASA made it to the moon because the moon was the goal. It wasn't simply the result of gradual technical improvements. The stretch goal itself had power.

Achieving a breakthrough means going beyond limits. Only after breaking through barriers that weren't meant to be broken and going beyond your own limits will you be able to see through to the next stage.

The problem is, the barriers themselves can be hard to see. Athletes aside, most of us don't think about the pursuit of our fullest potential and where our limits may be.

What is it that allows you to see your limits clearly? Goals.

On May 25, 1961, John F. Kennedy announced that the United States would land a man on the moon by the end of the 1960s. This was a response to the *Sputnik* crisis. *Sputnik* was the world's first artificial satellite, and it had been launched successfully by the Soviet Union. The United States had been outpaced. The thought that the Soviet Union, the hypothetical enemy, had overtaken the United States was a huge blow to American confidence. And just a month before Kennedy's address, the USSR had successfully launched a *manned* satellite into space. Yuri Gagarin became the first human being to look down on the Earth with his own eyes.

President Kennedy announced the plan to send a man to the moon to counter the widespread shock felt in the United States. His speech galvanized the American people. And the genius of it was that Kennedy set a time frame of nine years, telling the public that the United States would achieve the goal not "some-day," but "before this decade is out" (for more information, see https://er.jsc.nasa.gov/seh/ricetalk.htm).

The United States committed itself to sending a man to a heavenly body some 240,000 miles away when it was having trouble even launching satellites into orbit around Earth. And it was going to get that done in just nine years.

Common sense would say that it was impossible.

But that near impossibility instead made it a noble, heroic target.

Obviously, President Kennedy couldn't have been certain the goal would be achieved. But he probably thought he could prove it wasn't impossible.

Hearing of this seemingly impossible goal must have helped to make crystal clear the barriers blocking the way of the people working on the space program. I don't know if they faced dozens or hundreds of barriers, but I can say for certain that they overcame every one of them. They achieved dozens, perhaps hundreds, of breakthroughs, and on July 20, 1969, at 4:17 p.m. Eastern Daylight Time, *Apollo 11* landed on the moon.

Nothing is impossible. Inevitably, the impossible will become a possibility.

Humankind's future depends on how many people believe this, and the *Apollo 11* moon landing definitely created some believers.

It was achieved because President Kennedy set a clear, specific time frame of nine years, not simply because advances in aviation technology suddenly meant humankind could reach the moon.

This principle applies to all kinds of business, too. There is no such thing as aimless growth. There is no way that people or companies can truly grow if they simply plod along aimlessly doing routine work. Setting clear, specific goals and doing everything in your power to achieve them is essential for growth.

Set big goals. Set clear and specific goals with deadlines, and commit to achieving them. It's those goals that will generate transformational growth for you and for your company.

03 Learn the difference between a group and a team

You'll do your best work—by far—when you think of yourself as part of a team.

A group of thousands who merely carry out their assigned tasks is nothing more than a mob. It doesn't deserve to be called an organization. An organization must always strive to be more than just a random group completing predefined tasks. It must aim to be a team where members transcend individual roles and their efforts complement each other.

For practical reasons, roles and responsibilities have to be distributed when organizations become large. However, this often goes too far, especially in big organizations. Employees come to believe that their job is to simply fulfill the role they've been given. They even start to think that it's wrong for them to do anything that doesn't match their job description. This way of thinking is a destructive sickness.

Every business is at war in the effort to excel.

Since it's a competition, it's meaningless unless you win. To be certain of achieving victory, every member of your organization must work as though they themselves bear full responsibility for accomplishing the goals of the team. That is the moment at which a group evolves and can truly be called a team.

Here's one way I work to make that happen. At Rakuten, all employees clean their workplaces on Monday mornings. This has been the practice since the company had just a handful of employees.

It doesn't matter whether you are a new hire fresh out of college or a senior executive. We all clean our workplaces thoroughly. We all get down on our knees and polish our chair legs. We do this to remind ourselves that there's no aspect of the company's business that doesn't concern us.

The company's business is our business. From where you sit, do you believe this with all your heart? Those who don't will never succeed.

If you are a supervisor or a manager, you should never forget that winning hinges on whether you can bring together the people who work with you—to form that kind of team. If you are an employee, winning hinges on whether you can work as a member of your team, without ever losing focus. This is extremely important—important enough to transform your life.

If you think it's enough just to do the work you're paid for, and that doing any more is a waste of time, you're throwing your life down the drain. Working in this way is simply selling off chunks of your life—and our lives are not long enough for that. If you sell your life bit by bit, 30 to 40 years will go by before you know it.

New hires and junior employees should approach their work with the belief that they are key players who will take the company to new heights. An organization starts to realize its true potential when all team members share this belief. And when that happens, your own individual abilities will start to shine.

Even the best racecar driver won't win with an underperforming car. The relationship between individuals and a team is no different. You must not see yourself as alone, but as a part of a larger project. The key to realizing your full potential is working not in just any ordinary group but as part of an outstanding team.

04 Think about your mindset, skills, and knowledge

If you just daydream about success, you'll never actually be successful. Success doesn't depend on luck. You have to grab it with your own two hands.

There are only two types of people in this world: successful people and unsuccessful people. By definition, successful people succeed, while unsuccessful people never do. Successful people have three characteristics in common: mindset, skills, and knowledge.

When I say *mindset,* I mean your passion for work. Your mindset is the root of your motivation in the workplace. It could be the desire to succeed or to become rich, or a passion to satisfy your customers. Skills refers to your abilities. Communication and computer skills are useful in business. The ability to self-manage is also a skill. Then there's knowledge. It goes without saying that knowledge is useful in business. Truly capable people possess all three of these qualities.

However, few start out with a good balance of the three. Some might have a wealth of knowledge but lack the right mindset, for example. Or they might have the mindset but lack the skills. You need to objectively analyze yourself and figure out your areas of weakness. When you identify your weaknesses, you will also see ways to overcome them. If you overcome them, you are far more likely to succeed in business.

One word of caution for highly talented people: Talents are to a large extent innate. Outstanding communication abilities, for example, are often something you were born with. A person with that natural talent might become a salesperson—as an example—and achieve outstanding results right off the bat, without any special effort. You might say that individual has found his or her true calling, but actually there's a catch.

The catch is that it's difficult to achieve true success using only the talents you were born with. Without continuing to work to improve yourself, you cannot achieve true success.

Many who are blessed with natural talents don't study or make any extra effort, instead relying on those talents to get by. For whatever reason, people often quit studying the minute they enter the workforce—even though learning is so important, especially when you start out at work. If you don't have a wide array of natural talents, you can make up for most of that by studying and learning each day. There are plenty of outstanding salespeople, for example, who are not particularly talented conversationalists. In fact, it's not unusual to hear about outstanding, recognized salespeople who once struggled with their communication skills. They studied, practiced, and overcame their initial disadvantage.

I recall a colleague who took this approach. Early in the creation of Rakuten it became necessary for our company to work in a particular computer language, SQL. First, he acquired a beginner's book on SQL. Then, he hired a tutor. He was no longer in school, but he didn't let that stop him from learning. He sought the additional education he needed to acquire the necessary skill.

Certainly, this was also true for many Rakuten employees who worked here when I announced my plan to make English our company language. I called the process *Englishnization* and we set goals for every employee to meet. While many may have studied English in school, to pass a test and achieve the language levels we had set for employees, more study was necessary. Throughout Rakuten, employees formed study groups and conversation groups. Some used their vacation time to attend English language boot camps. It was a company-wide exercise in the value of additional study.

All these examples remind us that in business, you can overcome skill barriers through hard work and careful planning. You must keep accumulating knowledge and strive to improve yourself. Do not rely solely on your talents. New business ideas come out of analytical thinking and good judgment. While these are often considered inherent "talents," they can also be developed through daily training.

If you are conscious of this need to constantly grow and improve, you'll soon notice that even the newspapers and magazines you read every day are full of great ideas. Even something as simple as observing young people walking around town will give you new business ideas. I recall a time when I was on a business trip in Spain. I took a walk out to the local marketplace (mostly to try and counteract my bad case of jet lag). But as I strolled through the stalls, I was struck by the vivid colors and the impact these visual elements had on the shoppers around me. I came back from my trip with new ideas on how we could improve our website. Walking around had become part of my process for a successful redesign of our web page. With mindset, skills, and knowledge, the world presents unlimited possibilities for success.

05 Question yourself

Be humble, especially when you're successful.

Everything that exists will eventually cease to exist. Nothing is unchanging or permanent. Everything is transitory, including you and me.

In business, you should always bear this in mind, especially when work is going smoothly and you're feeling successful.

Individuals always grow confident when things go well. They start to think that they achieved success because they are special, because their way of doing things is the right way.

Obviously, there's nothing wrong with having confidence. But the time to leverage that confidence is when your work *isn't* going well. When you're surrounded by stiff competition and success seems out of reach, *that* is the time when you should be confident and walk with your head held high.

But when you actually achieve success, that's the time to shrug off your confidence.

Be humble enough to consider that you got lucky, that you happened to be in the right place at the right time. If circumstances change, you could be in trouble.

I'm not saying success is wholly due to luck. It might be 99 percent hard work. But if the remaining 1 percent doesn't go your way, things might end in disaster. And, in any case, you could still fail tomorrow.

That might make you feel extremely uncomfortable. But this is the kind of dynamic tension that drives people to work hard.

I feel much more uncomfortable when I notice people sitting back and basking in the glow of their own self-confidence.

No matter how solid your business model may seem, if you look 10 or 20 years ahead, you may find it's a house built on sand. Or worse, a house *made* of sand.

All business is just that fragile.

Society is like a river—it never stops flowing, even for a moment. The business climate continuously changes.

Businesses that are currently successful will inevitably fail. You must always prepare for the worst, based on this assumption.

Courage to question yourself is essential. Questioning yourself means examining *everything* about yourself, including the way you think, work, and live. It means questioning everything you have believed in until this moment.

I understand that this is really hard to do. But if you don't, you won't be able to create anything new. As long as you continue to cling to past success, you will never be able to achieve success in the future.

You must doubt yourself most when you are successful. You must accept that the way you do things is not the only way. You must have the courage, if a better way appears, to start from scratch.

Here's an example from my own experience. I founded Rakuten with the goal of being the world's No. 1 internet service company. That was the plan. That was our mantra for many years. As we grew, I saw that taking shape. We grew to be a leader in e-commerce, in fintech, in virtual communications, and entertainment. We were becoming everything we set out to be.

Then I began to think: Is that really our best ultimate goal? Or is that just an interim step for what Rakuten could ultimately become?

I did this thinking at a time when Rakuten was quite clearly successful. But it was in that success that I began to question myself. Was there a better way? A bigger goal? A new mantra?

I decided to make a shift. I created a new goal for Rakuten. The internet had become a given in our everyday lives, and I wanted us to think bigger than just internet services and think in broader terms. Our new vision was set for Rakuten to be a global innovation company. It's a shift in mindset and one that doesn't allow us to rest on our success in the internet services space. It pushes us all to think big and push ourselves to be true innovators in everything we do. In this context, we have explored new services and industries such as drone deliveries and cancer research, and we have reconfigured our thinking to focus not just on success in one industry but on innovation in everything we touch.

It was not easy to make that shift. I had more than one employee stand up during our weekly company meetings and question me. "I joined this company because the goal was to be the number one internet services company. What does this new goal mean?" I understood the sense of disruption and resistance to change. But I also knew that questioning our position, right at the moment of success, was a process that would push us into even greater opportunities.

Always keep your mind open to fresh possibilities and never stop looking for new directions and even better ways of doing things. That's the secret to sustainable growth.

06 A brand is a flag

When you run a company, you are doing more than just making money. You are assuming a role of leadership. When you are running a big company, you're doing this on a global scale.

Companies have started to resemble nations.

What is the essence of a nation? It's not its territory or currency. It's not even its people. Although these things determined national identity until the twentieth century, the advent of the internet means we must radically change how we think about countries, as any kind of information can now easily cross country borders and move freely from place to place.

Those who underestimate the power of the internet may say it's just a collection of data. And it's true that data are not physical entities but a product of our brains. However, by the same token, you could also say that currency, borders, and citizenship are just concepts thought up by humans. Everything that makes up the essence of a nation is information. And being information, it's affected by the internet. Building high walls at national borders might temporarily stop the flow of people and goods. But as long as the internet exists, it will be impossible to completely shut down the flow of information. Just as the Berlin Wall between East and West Germany was destroyed by their own citizens, borders will continue to be made obsolete by the flow of information.

It will be the same with currencies. The internet will make the concept of nations and their currencies ever weaker and more ambiguous, while corporations will become increasingly important. Consider the impact of companies such as Facebook and Google. These are companies with tremendous sway all over the world. Their users don't just treat them as services companies. In many ways, these companies are ecosystems informing societies within which their users live—much as individuals might once have thought of national borders. Customers of these global companies rely on them and integrate them into their daily lives. How companies of this stature behave has as much impact on users as the policies of their government.

As the presence of corporations in society becomes even more influential, the social responsibilities they assume will also grow. The pure pursuit of profit will not be enough to allow these companies to fulfill those weighty responsibilities.

It will be crucial for corporations of the future to commit to clearly setting out their ideals and ideologies—and to communicate a vision for the society that they are working toward. Whether or not a corporation can spell out that vision will determine its scope for growth.

In that sense, I believe your brand is as powerful as any national flag.

Rakuten flies a flag that represents empowerment of individuals, business, and society via the internet. We strongly believe that supporting the talents and efforts of individuals and groups using the internet to realize their dreams is at the heart of our mission. That empowerment allows all of us to push the boundaries of our individual and corporate identities and will lead to a happier, more prosperous society.

If you're working for a company, do you know what your company flag embodies in spirit? If you do, and if you believe in the ideals it represents, you should give it your all to uphold them. If what the flag represents is unclear, then you should create a new one. It doesn't have to be created by management. If management won't clarify the company's principles, flying a flag based on a consensus among its employees will do. The time has passed when individuals offered their whole lives to companies without giving deeper thought to the firm's ideals or convictions.

Branded products will come to represent their owners' ideals rather than their wealth or social status. Individuals will "vote" through their consumption activity: companies that win the support of large numbers of people will grow significantly and their ideals will change society. Companies must therefore take great care of those brands that carry as much pride as any nation's flag at the Olympics.

07 The internet transformation continues

Think boldly about the future. In the age of the internet, change is a given.

It's true that no one knows what will happen tomorrow. However, we'll never be able to shape the future if we don't try to see what it looks like through the haze of uncertainty.

When I established Rakuten Ichiba in 1997, I drew up four hypotheses about the internet:

1. It will become simpler and more convenient.
2. It will spread like wildfire.
3. Consumers in Japan and beyond will buy things by using it.
4. It will change the retail industry.

All four are now true.

Some self-proclaimed experts might say that all four of these were obvious from the time the internet started, that they don't even deserve the name *hypotheses* because anyone with even a little knowledge of the internet could have seen they were bound to come true.

But if it was all so obvious, why didn't they do the same thing I did?

I'm not boasting about my foresight. I'm trying to say that only a few dare to think boldly about the future.

Many can come up with explanations for things that have already happened, but they do not even try to focus their attention on the future. Many around us like to say you can't even know what will happen tomorrow. I don't think they're being circumspect. I believe they're being lazy. Rather than trying to analyze the secret of Rakuten's growth over the past 20 years, you should apply those powers of analysis to the next 10. If you do this, you'll realize there is one thing that we can say for certain about the future: although the internet has radically changed society, the changes so far have been nothing compared to the ones that lie ahead. The internet will continue to transform the world. Those engaged in business should constantly bear this in mind.

What kind of society will human beings create through this revolution? I believe business holds the key. People once created new orders via politics and war. That era is passing. Fueled by the transformative powers of the internet, business will challenge national and government hegemony. Business creativity—the economic activity generated by the actions of everyone alive on the earth today—will create the new order.

08 The internet will curate the world's knowledge and data, but the human touch will still be key

No matter how far technology advances, people will be attracted to services that have a human touch.

The internet's essential function is to connect all of humanity's knowledge and information.

Obviously, human beings had tools to do this before the internet was invented, notably speech and writing. Through the tool of language, human beings have shared knowledge and information.

It is thanks to this ability that human beings, relatively weak animals, have overpowered other creatures, and now reign over the Earth. From letters and books to telecommunications, language has made it possible to share knowledge and information widely and precisely.

The internet is merely an extension of this.

However, as a "technology" for sharing knowledge and information, the invention of the internet reaches a whole different dimension because, at least in theory, it can connect all of our knowledge and information, unhindered by spatial limitations.

This is awesome. It sounds like science fiction—by connecting to the internet, a single individual can access the collective intelligence of the entire human race. This is leading us into a period of tremendous innovation. From drones to cars to IBM's super computer Watson, collective intelligence is guiding us forward in new ways.

That said, simply bringing together vast amounts of information is meaningless.

If the information isn't organized and indexed, it has no more meaning than a mountain of trash. Without the technology to instantly find a single needle among haystacks upon haystacks of data, the internet would be far less useful. In this sense, Google has played a huge role. With apologies to developers of competing search engines, I'd say the internet would never have become as important as it is today if it weren't for Google.

Looking further ahead, though, search engines will become obsolete. No matter how advanced the search engine, as long as it is an automated system, it will eventually become a common, everyday product we take for granted, like a telephone or a washing machine. The praise that has been heaped on Google is similar to the way previous generations talked about the makers of the first cars. The company is held in such high regard because no other current "automobile" is as advanced as Google's. As soon as another with the same performance comes along, Google's relative advantage in the market will decline. This is a limitation of the tech industry: the more useful a tool, the faster it will be copied, and the faster people will strive to better it.

Tapping into human desires will be crucial to the continued success of the internet businesses. We tend to forget this because of our focus on rapidly advancing technology. But it's precisely because we live in such a technological age that you can't stand out or beat the competition with technology alone.

We've seen that in our own business. With products like Viber, a voice and messaging mobile app, and Viki, an entertainment platform, it has not been as much about inventing new technology tools, but about offering emotional satisfaction. Viki does not just host entertainment. Our product managers strive to create communities for fans and to connect fans around the world—using entertainment to build connections and friendships across borders. In that way, Viki is not just a tech tool; it is a human connection machine.

Rakuten Ichiba is built on a myriad of human stories. We started out with the concept that merchants who freely created their own original content and succeeded in delivering a message with emotional resonance would have the opportunity to reach their customers in a way that more streamlined, standardized e-commerce models never would. We often compared our marketplace to that of an outdoor market, where you can enjoy browsing and interacting with the stallholders, while our competitors are more likely to be pursuing a vending machine model, where customers hit a standard-size button and receive the product as depicted on its glass front.

Times may change, but you will never be successful in business without touching people's hearts.

09 Taking action leads to deeper thinking

In business, rather than spending time thinking about this and that, you have to do something. Nothing will ever happen if all you do is think about things.

Of course you can't help having some thoughts about things before you act. I'm not saying don't think at all. Actually, nothing is more important than thinking. It's impossible to achieve business success without thinking, and it goes without saying that in business the better thinkers succeed.

What I'm trying to say is that in order to really think, you have to take action.

If you are only taking action after thinking, you are on the wrong track. You should be taking action in order to think things through. That's the right perspective.

Reality as you perceive it only starts to mean something when there is feedback *from* that reality. In other words, thoughts only start to mean something as a result of action. It is a virtuous cycle that can lead to great results.

For example, trying to teach a person who's never held a racket to play tennis using words alone is ridiculous. It makes no intuitive sense. You should hand them the racquet and the ball, have them watch others, then let them hit the ball themselves. Teaching someone to play tennis after they have tried is a far more efficient method of teaching.

It's exactly the same in business.

Despite this, many people spend all their time thinking about things and theorizing, without actually taking any actions. Sometimes I wonder if these people are using "thinking" as an excuse not to do anything.

It goes without saying that in the world of business, action carries various kinds of risk. It's natural to hesitate before acting. But this is precisely why you should act to think.

I don't mean big actions, necessarily. Just big enough to get you thinking. For example, say you come up with a business model. First develop it on a small scale, and base your thinking on the results. This kind of small experiment is crucial to success in business. A single experiment is far more valuable as a point of reference than a mass of information, no matter how hard it was to acquire.

It's fine to start small, but first you must act. Then think. Then take the next step, then think again, then act again.

Businesses are built on this step-by-step process.

Suppose you throw a ball against a wall and want to know how it will bounce back. You could predict the ball's trajectory using equations of motion, but real walls are uneven. They have pits and bumps. In the real world, balls don't always bounce back as theory predicts.

Of course you could factor in the unevenness, the pits, and the bumps, but rather than spending all that time on such a complex calculation, why not just throw the ball at the wall? You would learn much more that way—and have a lot more fun!

I'll tell you another secret.

When you throw the ball at the wall, don't be afraid that it might bounce back in an unexpected direction. More often than not, an unexpected bounce reveals an opportunity to improve yourself or your process. I had that experience when I tried to purchase TBS, a Japanese television network, long before the entertainment industry began its shift online. I was certain that the rise of the internet would revolutionize entertainment, and that Rakuten and TBS would form a formidable partnership when that time came. But the ball bounced back to me in an unexpected way when the leadership of TBS did not share my vision of the future of the internet. They saw the event as a hostile takeover. They fought the change and in the end, I was unable to convince them that my offer would be beneficial to all. I lost money and was roundly criticized by media at the time.

How can that bad bounce be an opportunity? It has served to remind me ever since that no matter how good a deal looks "by the numbers," there will always be a human element that must be considered. That bad bounce helped me to craft better business plans. I was always mindful after that experience that the emotional reaction of the company leadership will be a factor that I must consider going into any business deal.

Here is another example: I had—and missed—the opportunity to invest early on in Uber. I was not convinced initially of the investment's possibilities. As Uber stock took off, it was clear that my outlook had been overly pessimistic. But that bounce ultimately paid off for me. Because it focused my attention on the true potential of ridesharing, and when another investment opportunity came along, I was ready. At a Silicon Valley office, I met with some members of my team and the founders of Lyft, a new ridesharing firm. When the meeting was over, I turned to my Rakuten team members right in that moment and told them I was a yes. The unexpected bounce on Uber had revealed to me the potential of the expanding *sharing economy*. When the next opportunity arose, I did not hesitate.

Thinking is good. But it's action that will stimulate your thinking.

10 Continuously improve by a fraction. It's the key to what others call "good luck"

You can make your own luck.

When someone is successful, people often envy their "good luck." I understand this feeling, but people who think that success depends on luck will never be successful themselves. When a big opportunity presents itself, you won't be able to seize it unless you are ready for it. In fact, you probably won't even recognize it.

A person who has never learned to surf won't be able to ride a wave, whatever its size. While it may be true that Rakuten rode the dot-com bubble to success, those who were unprepared for it saw it as an unmitigated disaster. Riding great waves of opportunity requires careful preparation.

The problem, then, is what kind of preparation is needed. I believe it's simply a matter of small, everyday improvements.

It's not enough to just work diligently every day. You have to make progress, any progress at all. Be a little better today than yesterday, a little better tomorrow than today. However high the mountain, the climber must start by putting one foot in front of the other. In business, you must improve the quality of your work every day, even if by only 0.1 percent. If you improve by just 0.1 percent per day, after a year you will be 44 percent better at what you do. This accumulation of improvement will lead to success. Only those who maintain this kind of effort can ride the waves of opportunity.

So first, get into the habit of looking at your own work from another person's perspective. It's easy to find faults in other people's work, because you can look at it objectively. Turn that objective eye on yourself. You'll probably find many things that should be improved.

Obviously, there's a reason for each fault. Maybe you didn't have enough time, or enough help, or it was just too much work. When you see these faults in others' work, you think they should be able to fix them easily. But it doesn't seem so easy when you look at your own problems, does it? Sadly, everyone feels like this.

Nevertheless, a little effort can make a big difference. If you feel you don't have any time, get up earlier and get to your desk even just 10 minutes earlier than the day before. That's one example of a 0.1 percent improvement.

The crucial thing is to keep making 0.1 percent improvements every day. Don't just do them when you think of them. Create a *shikumi*—a system that allows you to build on each day's efforts.

Specifically, keep a record so that you can look at your work objectively on the shortest possible timescale. I recommend keeping a daily record. We do this at Rakuten. In the early years of my company, every day I received a three-ringed binder holding printouts of all the Rakuten businesses and their results for that day. Now, of course, we collect that data and deliver it digitally. I see the way our businesses are functioning in real time. I'm able to see the raw data and look for trends or problems. You can do this in your own work. A short timescale means it doesn't take long to fill in. You can see at a glance whether you have continued to accumulate these daily 0.1 percent improvements.

It may seem like a mundane task, but if you do it every day, this mundane task will lead to great results.

Improving productivity by fractions is an essential secret to riding big waves of opportunity, and becoming a "lucky" person.

2

Personal Development

Understanding who you are is the first step to success. Know your weak points, and think about how you can continue to grow.

11 Push yourself like a professional (athlete) does

Be passionately professional about your job, no matter what it is.

People who enjoy their job more than anything else are the ones who can be called true professionals. They love it so much that they think about their job all the time, all year round, no matter what they're doing. There's no need to teach people like that the secrets of success—they're already successful. Consider an athlete like Jack Nicklaus and you can see what a lifetime of professional level effort can do, both on and off the golf course. This kind of athlete is a passionate professional.

There's nothing better than a life given meaning by the joy of work. I'd go so far as to say that we are born into this world to work. The problem is what to do when you just can't think of your work in those terms. In fact, to a certain degree, this mental challenge applies to all of us.

Perhaps you're not passionate about your current job. Or maybe you'd really prefer to be doing something else. There are lots of different reasons why this happens, but before you spend time considering all those different reasons to leave, first try putting your all into the work you are doing right now. After having put all your energies into the job you have today, if you still think it's not what you want to do, then—and only then—you should consider changing careers or starting your own business.

If you bail out before giving your whole-hearted all to that job you have now, then you'll likely find yourself in the same situation in your next job, too. There's an old saying that if someone does something once, they will do it again and again. The truth is, those who can succeed in one job may be able to achieve success in any job, while those who can't succeed in one job may never succeed.

So the first step is to become obsessed with the job at hand. It's not as hard as it sounds. Just think of work as a game. At the risk of inviting misunderstanding, I must admit that I feel like my work is the greatest game ever. Nothing is more fascinating to me. I'm so obsessed with it, I'll sometimes forget to eat or sleep.

And what is the essence of a game? It's about creating targets and achieving them.

Creating targets is the first secret to enjoying your job. To achieve your goals, you need to bring your wisdom and ingenuity to bear. I believe all people want to see their ideas and their creative efforts at work in the real world. The more you're able to do this, the more enjoyable your job will become.

It's the people whose passion for their work wins them the respect of their peers who, whether they realize it or not, are continuously setting targets and working out ingenious ways to achieve them. Enjoying your work may actually hinge on whether or not you are consistently working to hit targets.

A person who feels no passion for his work is like an archer with a bow and arrow but no target. No matter how many times the archer draws his bow and shoots his arrows, with nothing to aim at, he'll never enjoy the sport of archery. He will never hit a bull's-eye because there isn't one in his sights.

How to motivate yourself is a challenge we all face. If you think your job is boring, set yourself targets. Aim at those targets and fire off your arrows. If you hit your target, you'll feel good. If you don't, you'll feel frustrated. You'll start wanting to hit those bull's-eyes all the time. You'll think up creative ways to do it, and you'll work hard to make it happen. All of us can experience this chain reaction. This is the essence of finding meaning in your work.

12 Play catch between your left and right brain

When forming an opinion or hatching a new idea, engage your left brain and right brain in a mental game of catch.

They say the right side of the brain controls intuition, the left side language and logic. Thinking objectively about how I come up with ideas and my process of turning them into specific plans or business models, this seems pretty accurate.

Ideas that arise in the right side of the brain are vague in terms of details, even if the outline is clear. In this sense, they can be extremely simple. Even if intuitively you know the idea is correct, you cannot communicate it effectively because it's not yet been put into words. It's the role of the left side of the brain to turn these vague concepts into words. And turning them into words means placing them within a framework. As a result of this, ideas that arise in the right side of your brain always shrink to some extent. On the other hand, when those ideas are weighed against existing business frameworks and the vague details are clarified by words, ideas that were simple can become quite complex. This repeated exchange between the left and right sides of your brain is like a game of catch. You toss ideas that were put into words and made more complex in the left side of the brain back to the right side brain for an intuitive judgment. And you repeat this process again and again.

I'll give you a specific example. You're drinking a particular wine and you think it tastes wonderful. You start to wonder why it tastes so good. You think perhaps it's because the grapes were harvested in a particular year from a particular vineyard and the tannins have mellowed just the right amount, giving the wine a full-bodied flavor. Having analyzed the wine, you take another sip and try to determine whether the flavor is really due to the tannins having mellowed. At this point, you might realize that it's not just the tannins. The bouquet is excellent as well. You realize you haven't put some characteristics of the wine into words. Then you start to think about why the bouquet is so good.

This process, in which you intentionally use the opposing functions of the two sides of the brain (i.e., intuition and analysis) is what brainstorming is all about. As you play more catch, the inner exchange becomes sharpened. The ball hits the mitt with a crisp popping sound. Speed and focus are improved since the tosses travel at high speed once you are deep in thought.

Taking a simple idea and complicating it, then simplifying it, and complicating it again makes it possible to identify the core of the idea. It allows you to clearly see the "roots" of the idea, as well as the "leaves and branches."

In my case, after playing this game of catch for a while, I reach a point where suddenly everything becomes crystal clear. It feels like you suddenly know exactly where all the pieces of a jigsaw puzzle need to go to complete the puzzle. The left and right brain perform a triple play with laser timing and precision. It's like in this moment, all at once, I can see exactly where and when every moving part should be, with that crystal clarity.

It was like this when I developed the idea for Rakuten Ichiba. I understood what the core, or the trunk, of the business would be, what the roots were that would support that trunk, and how the branches and leaves should look. I could even see how that vision would change in the future and how we'd have to change and adapt to that. It was as if I was standing high up on a mountain looking down on Rakuten Ichiba now and in the future. I could see it so clearly, I could almost touch it. That was more than 20 years ago now.

Many people will readily take an idea and create a business model around it. But I doubt there are as many people who will then reassess their model from an intuitive perspective to see if it will really work. But not doing this makes it much harder to bring that idea to life.

Don't allow your idea to flow in just one direction, from the right side to the left side of your brain. Toss it back and forth between the two sides. This is the secret to successfully landing your business idea.

13 Plan forward from birth or backward from death

Write your bio. Now, use your imagination and write your obituary. Think about how your life looks from both those perspectives.

Right now, you're alive. But one day you'll die. And although nothing is more certain than that, it's only human nature to avoid thinking about our own mortality too many times a day. We rationalize that there's no point in thinking about death because we don't know when it will come. As Steve Jobs famously said, "No one wants to die."

We don't know when the end will come, but come it will. What do any of us want to achieve in the time we are given? To think about our plans for life, we should first think deeply about how the end should look because this is the reality that awaits us. Addressing this first will make it much easier to see exactly what any one of us should be doing now.

Regardless of what you're planning, you can't really call it a plan unless it has a timeline. It's lonely and terrifying to think about one's end, but you can't truly plan your life without starting there. It's also true that those who are unable to make a genuine plan for their own life will also be unable to achieve anything that is genuinely great.

My own personal reflections on death emerged from the 1995 Hanshin-Awaji Earthquake. My parents' home in the city of Akashi was badly damaged, and I lost my aunt and uncle, who were both very dear to me. It's hard to put into words how I felt as I wandered through the mountains of rubble in my hometown searching for signs of them, and then when I finally found both my aunt and uncle laid out in a school gymnasium. They were placed alongside the bodies of so many people who had been healthy and happy until the day before, when the quake struck, and had all lost their lives in an instant.

That image is etched in my memory. I can't get away from it. I came to know just how fleeting life is, not through words but through a sadness so crushing that I thought it would tear at my heart forever. I also understood, deep down within my body and soul, that my life too is ephemeral and all that much more precious as a consequence.

Of course, some people would say that they have no interest in achieving great things. I'm comfortable with their decision—and I genuinely mean that. Happiness is not just a matter of great achievements, and not everyone should feel compelled to believe it's the only reason to live.

But, in my case, I want to achieve something great as proof that I existed. It's a way of showing my appreciation for all of the opportunities I have received over the years. My dream is to create a system through which every person in the world can achieve happiness. If I'm going to achieve this goal, I must never forget that my time is limited.

They say the sixteenth-century warlord Oda Nobunaga was fond of a line from the play *Atsumori*: "Human life lasts only 50 years." He was acutely aware that our time to have impact in this life is limited. He saw his own window of opportunity as finite, and I think he too must have must have thought about life working backward from death. It is a mindset that reminds you to waste no time.

14 Create an objective personality when you're in the hot seat

The next time you find yourself in a drama, consider how it may look from the perspective of the audience.

"Objective personality" is an expression I coined to simply mean taking an objective, third-party perspective of yourself.

People tend to make odd decisions during times of crisis, as they do when retreating from a difficult situation. Those bad decisions often then compound the damage even further. We've all seen business and political leaders during times of crisis. We may be sitting home, glued to our televisions, wondering why they behave the way they do—often making their own situations worse. But the fact is that in situations like that you can lose sight of the things that seem obvious to everyone else on this side of the television cameras, or a more objective viewpoint. When you are backed into a corner, it's not an exaggeration to say that the damage caused by poor judgment in such crises often causes more damage than the initial crisis itself.

That's why we must face each challenge objectively, from the perspective of the person at home, watching it on TV. When we examine something from the point of view of a bystander, we may make different choices. Think of it this way: We may make a big deal out of a splinter when it's in our own little finger. But if you think of it as someone else's finger, you may realize how ridiculous it is to make a fuss.

This outsider perspective may help you keep your emotions under control. A situation you see as a crisis may actually be much less alarming if you think about the problem as if it were someone else's. It's the same when you're worrying over something. If you take a bystander perspective, you may soon realize that many of those worries are not worth worrying about at all.

It's clear which of the two perspectives will be most useful when you're trying to address an urgent problem. When you're upset or in trouble, try taking yourself out of the picture and thinking about how to deal with it from an outsider's point of view. This is the best way to deal with a crisis.

Of course, this is easier said than done. Especially when you're in a really tight spot, it's almost impossible to take that perspective straight away. So I recommend that you practice this even when you're not stuck in a difficult spot. Try to imagine how others perceive you. In fact, dry runs of this sort can also be useful for improving your attitude and people skills.

One more important point about taking this alternative perspective: When others are faced with a difficult situation, try imagining how you would feel if it were happening to you. If you can imagine someone else's pain, the ability to empathize will lead you to the right decisions. If you feel the pain when someone else has cut their little finger as if you were feeling it yourself, you'll know what you should do. What might look to someone else like a small pain can be pure agony for the person experiencing it directly.

With that perspective in mind, reach out to help others in trouble as much as you can. Doing this will mean better relationships with your team, at home, and also positively contribute to business relationships with clients and customers.

15 Never stop learning. Ever

"Study all the time. Study everything."

This was the advice of one of my favorite professors at college. It's a lesson I really took to heart. I'm impatient by nature so I never had much time for the hard grind of study. I hate long, tedious tasks so I knew I was always going to cram for tests by staying up the whole night before.

When I was a student, I studied because I had to, cramming overnight or just before final exams. But when you enter the workforce, many people think that studying was something they did in college. In truth, learning is a never-ending project. In fact, it's much more important than when you were a student. People quit studying because there's no pressing need, like a test exam hanging over their head. This is a big problem.

You'd never come across a professional athlete who's quit practicing because they've turned pro. Their personal efforts are magnified the moment it is their path to make a living. The moment they stop training is the moment they cease to excel professionally. Some may think what they learned at school hasn't helped them at all in their working lives. But the reason it hasn't helped them is because they stopped studying the instant they entered the workforce. The most important reason we study at school is to learn how to study. If you don't study, then obviously you won't be able to use that skill. Forgetting how to study after you went to all the trouble of learning that skill is an enormous waste of time and effort.

What you choose to study will differ according to the individual, but you should continue to study your entire life. If you don't continually absorb new ways of doing things and improve yourself, your own development will come to a dead end. Those who put their all into critical analytical thinking in school will understand the power of studying something systematically. After all, with just eight years of study, a high school senior will suddenly become a qualified lawyer or a doctor, even if they're just starting out.

In the middle of our Englishnization efforts at Rakuten to make English the corporate language, I felt comfortable in English so I decided to take up Chinese. It's a challenging language and very different from Japanese, but when I stood on the stage for the launch of our Kobo eBooks service in Taiwan and made some simple remarks in Chinese, I felt an immediate warm and positive response from the guests assembled that made my efforts worthwhile.

If you seriously dedicate yourself to lifelong learning, you can change who you are. If you do that, your work will become more enjoyable, and because of that, you'll want to study more. Those who've internalized that cycle will achieve significant growth as talented members of the workforce. They'll have the capacity to achieve extraordinary things at work. Make time for study to improve yourself, be it only 30 minutes to an hour in your day. The accumulation of this time will determine who you are three to five years from now.

Of course, studying isn't only something you do at a desk. It's important to be aware that absolutely everything you experience is a form of study. You can learn things from your day-to-day work. Accumulating such institutional knowledge and adding to your mastery of various skills can only make you invaluable to others.

You'll be incredibly bored for your entire life if you've decided your main goal at work is simply to get through the daily routine. But if you strive to learn something from work, that will fuel your personal growth. No matter what the job, the joy of personal growth will enable you to give it your all.

We are born into this world to learn. Personal growth is the greatest joy of life. So, never stop learning. Ever.

16 Build self-confidence through small successes
Make a habit of achieving the goals you have set yourself.

Even the best mountain climbers didn't start with the world's tallest peaks. They started with small mountains, then moved on to larger ones. While it's important to set big goals, if the goals you set are too ambitious, you'll lose heart along the way.

The better path is a series of successes, however small they may be. This will help you achieve your dreams and look fondly back at the small incremental steps that made them happen. And nothing fuels more successes than a series of victories that you can draw upon to push you forward

The feeling of elation when things go well and the feeling of accomplishment when you achieve a success are both joys that are hard to beat. These joys will give you the strength of mind to devote the effort, and bear the suffering, that their achievement requires. It's the source of the energy one needs to persevere even when the going gets tough.

When you get tired of your job or can't put everything into it, it's because you have not yet experienced the joy of success that awaits you on the other side of all your hard work.

Initially, climbing even a 1,000-meter mountain won't be easy. And you'll probably be overjoyed the first time you reach the summit. However, the next time you reach that same summit, the emotion won't be as intense. You'll probably want to climb a taller mountain to once again feel that intense sense of accomplishment as you reach a new peak. You'll climb 2,000 meters, then 3,000 meters, then even higher.

As you build a series of successes, you will begin to eye more ambitious goals. Reaching the highest goal you set for yourself will continue to reinforce your inner self-confidence. The tallest peaks in the world lie at the end of this personal journey.

They say the best hitters in baseball repeatedly watch video footage of themselves pounding good hits and blasting home runs. They don't watch footage of themselves striking out because that repetition doesn't reaffirm how to achieve success. Instead, this visual image of success is what they want to constantly replay in their memories, so they can draw upon both the mental and physical preparations that led to it.

Nothing is impossible if you can learn this mental discipline.

When you understand this, not just cognitively but with every inch of your being, you'll see what you're really capable of. Then, one day, you'll find a deeper purpose centered around these moments of success. Discovery of that purpose will be the tallest peak in your future.

17 Always be curious and ambitious

Occupational burnout is not simply about working too hard. It can also be about losing a sense of intellectual curiosity and personal ambition.

Many will decide on a goal—to enter a top university or to pass a notoriously difficult exam—and work single-mindedly to achieve it. This laser-focused drive isn't bad in itself. The challenge comes when laser focus promotes inflexibility and narrows your thinking about the world around you.

Heaven is not waiting at the top of that mountain. The only things at the top of a mountain are the view and the satisfaction of having completed the ascent.

The top of the world may offer a more spectacular view and greater satisfaction than you could ever imagine, but at the end of the day, however stunning that is, it's still just a view and sense of satisfaction, nothing more. However much they love mountains, no climber lives at the summit. The summit is usually considered the goal, and climbing is the means of achieving it. But actually it's the other way around. The peak is not the real goal, climbing is. The peak merely provides the motivation to climb.

Goals in life and business are not the same as mountain peaks, but their place in an individual's experience is similar. You need to set goals to continue to work hard every day. A marathon without a finish line would be tough. So we set goals. However, in real life and work, you can't stop running when you've reached a goal. You must set a new one.

Curiosity and the drive to improve provide the energy that keeps people running. Running becomes harder when this energy begins to fade. Ensuring that your curiosity doesn't wither away is another reason you need to learn continuously, even after you enter the workforce.

The world is full of surprises. As long as you don't give up trying to absorb and learn from these surprises, you'll stay curious. If you're curious, you will not be deterred when the surprises are roadblocks in your path.

Always know who your rivals are, and their strengths, because this will also fuel your drive to improve. It's a big world out there. No matter how much you improve, there will still always be someone out there ahead of you. When you tire, remember there's always someone working harder than you. And don't forget that the greater your effort, the greater the joy that awaits on the other side.

Nothing in life or work is ever complete. You can at some point say you've done enough and stop, but you'll never reach a point where everything is done.

How you see this—as a source of pain or inspiration—can put you on one of two completely different paths.

Will you live in a dream-state hell, where you must run forever, or in a goal-inspired heaven, where you can run as far as you like and count your successes? It depends entirely on your curiosity and ambition.

18 Find a partner to play intellectual "catch" with

Just as pro baseball players play catch to warm up and check their form, you can bounce ideas off a colleague to test your own judgment about how to solve a problem.

As well as playing catch with the left and right sides of your brain, it's also important to play catch with others. Playing mental catch with a colleague is a little bit different from just seeking out advice.

I do this all the time to sort out my thoughts when I'm perplexed about something and can't come up with an answer, or when I get a new idea. It is usually then that I notice the problems in the way I'm approaching the situation.

There are times, of course, when the conclusion remains the same even after a good round of intellectual catch. In fact, this is usually the case. But the interaction will make you feel differently. First, there's meaning in putting your thoughts into words and sharing them with others. Even if the person you're talking to disagrees with you, and you're not convinced by their argument, it's immensely valuable to discover what alternative opinions may exist.

There are also many times I realize my own mistakes when hearing my explanation in the context of conversation. And there are times when, although I was previously unable to come up with any ideas, good ones arise as the conversation progresses. Fuzzy thoughts crystalize into concrete concepts and form the bedrock on which to build an entirely new solution.

In contrast to someone you have to consult in a formal way, a catch partner you can talk to about your problems at any time—in the way you would play a casual game of passing a ball back and forth—is an invaluable treasure.

The best way to find that partner is by starting to play. Try tossing a verbal "ball" to someone near you by starting the conversation. People are strange creatures. If you toss them a ball, they'll usually toss it back. That's where the game starts. This is much more constructive than gossiping about your boss or coworkers. Even more importantly, finding a good partner for playing catch makes life more fun.

One advantage of startup culture is that there's always someone to play catch with. Starting a company is a process of trial and error. Before each iteration, there's a lively discussion with those close to you. In the early days of Rakuten, playing catch was something that took place naturally in the tight quarters shared by our small team. There were only a few employees in a small office, so we basically played catch 24/7. It's no exaggeration to say Rakuten was born from those spontaneous conversations that took place every day.

We still engage in this same exercise—on a larger scale—even today. The number of employees has grown and so has the company, and it's become harder to talk to employees whenever I want. But I still play catch every chance I get. For example, the best way to find out what's popular today is to play catch with younger employees. You get a much more genuine feeling this way than from looking at survey results, for example. You can read faces, take the temperature of the room, and see authentic reactions play out in front of you.

That natural communication, that doesn't rely on the internet, will become more and more important for corporations. In this sense, playing catch is also an important communication tool.

Of course, playing catch isn't limited to the workplace. My wife has long been an important catch partner for me. My late father was also one of my best catch partners. A respected economist, he was always willing to jump in and challenge my assumptions. Nothing is more useful than having a catch partner who points out things you don't realize and isn't afraid to say things you don't want to hear. Find someone you can play catch with at any time in order to objectively understand your own way of thinking and how to do your job efficiently, with lasting impact.

19 Set clear goals for your actions

Building a game plan for self-improvement is critical to growth. So is an incremental series of improvements to any product. In increments is how we do everything at Rakuten.

That said, words like "improvement" and "growth" are abstract concepts that often need to be grounded. Simply advocating at a conceptual level is meaningless unless you translate your ideas into specific targets and concrete actions you can take.

For example, at Rakuten we implemented what we called the *One-Eighth Project*. It was an initiative to eliminate time wasted in meetings.

Our solution was simple. First, we halved the number of meetings. Then we halved the number of participants taking part in meetings. Then we halved the length of meetings. Half of half of half is one-eighth. In this way we were able to reduce the amount of time spent in meetings to a noticeably small fraction of what it was before.

If "reduce time spent in meetings" had simply been a slogan, nothing would have changed. But because we took concrete steps, the time spent in meetings was actually reduced.

Reduce waste! Save electricity! Be kind to the elderly! Save the Earth! Slogans abound. But no matter how well-intentioned those who shout them may be, following them up with action and specific targets is what leads to sustained progress.

Training regimes for top athletes are always specific and clear. The goal of the training is always itemized and tracked. The impact of strength training is much greater if the athlete knows which muscle is being exercised.

If this is true for strength training, it's even more important to take focused action in business. It's not enough just to say you'll do your best or work hard.

You must take specific action, bearing in mind the reason you're doing the job and the results it will lead to. Abstract action will lead only to abstract results. You won't get anywhere if you don't have a clear destination.

I took this to heart when we rolled out the plan to make English our official company language. When I made the announcement that we would undertake Englishnization, it came with specific targets. We set goals, that in a certain period of time every employee should be able to achieve a certain score on TOEIC. This was not easy for many employees. Many had studied English in school, but to rise to the level of using English every day in the workplace was a huge task. Still, if I had said, "Let's all try very hard to speak English at work," I believe we would not have been successful. Only by setting concrete targets was the transition to English made possible.

It's said that a journey of a thousand miles begins with a single step.

But the bigger question is: No matter whether you are taking major strides or baby steps, are you heading toward your goal? If you set targets to measure your success, your actions will become more meaningful.

20 Remember that great information can come from surprising places

You never can tell where great information might come from. We are trained as business leaders to look at traditional sources for information—the media, academia, industry, and research. But if we understand that great information—even inspiration— can come to us anywhere, anytime, we open ourselves to ideas we might otherwise have missed.

When you are open to information in all its forms, you understand your world in a new way. For example, in his *Book of Five Rings,* legendary swordsman Musashi Miyamoto compares the jobs of a carpenter and a samurai, noting that many of the basic behaviors of tool maintenance, focus, and attention to detail are similar in both professions. Strategy, he concludes, is not just a war game but a way of life that must be practiced, much as an artisan would. In thinking about battle strategy, but looking to a profession many would consider far from the battlefield, the author gleaned a new way to hone his own craft, by watching the work of another.

There are many examples of information arriving to us in surprising ways. We've all heard the famous story about Isaac Newton discovering the laws of gravity after watching an apple fall from a tree. Some say that story was actually made up some time later. True or not, people love the story because it contains a mysterious truth about the creative process. Answers and ideas are often hidden in places that at first seem completely unrelated. To put it another way, nothing is ever completely irrelevant. All information is valuable.

Answers and ideas may not always be apparent, but no one is hiding them from you. It's just that you don't see them. Look for them and you'll find them.

To develop the ability to uncover hidden information, you have to engage the world with curiosity. Be interested in everything. Then, you need to look for the true nature of things.

But this alone is not enough. Because no matter how hard you look, you won't see anything unless you're actively tackling problems within yourself.

When you get really immersed in something, you'll think about it whatever you're doing. Only then will everything you see and hear around you become your teacher.

It's like when you're in love. Everyone may have experienced this: You think about the person you're in love with wherever you are and whatever you're doing. It's a similar mental state.

So, speaking poetically, becoming sensitive to all kinds of information means the same as to fall in love with your job. If you experience, even just once, being so caught up in your job that you can't eat or sleep, and all you do is wonder how to tackle the challenges you're facing, then you'll come to understand what I mean when I say that "everything can be a source of valuable information."

There are some fundamental differences between work and love. Sometimes love doesn't lead anywhere, no matter how obsessed you are. But that's not the case with work. With work, if you really think hard enough about something, you'll always find an answer.

Become sensitive to all kinds of information so you don't miss anything. Musashi Miyamoto got ideas from watching carpenters because he spent all his time thinking about what it means to be a warrior. Had Isaac Newton not been obsessed with physics, he wouldn't have given any thought to the falling apple. Everything becomes a hint if you're tackling a problem that you can't solve no matter how hard you try. Answers are hidden in everything.

21 Don't rationalize your behavior as others do

Humans will go to great lengths to rationalize their behavior, even when it's to their own detriment. This is a lesson I've learned myself many times, by observing my own actions.

The need to justify yourself is the single greatest hindrance to logical thinking. Sometimes I wonder if most of our misjudgments can be traced back to this single impulse.

No matter how great or admired a person is, at some point they have made very obvious mistakes. It doesn't matter if they are admired as literary figures, empathetic political leaders or dynamic inventors creating transformational products. They are like all of us, and we have all made mistakes, some larger than others. The common denominator for all humans is the innate desire to deflect blame away from ourselves, rather than owning our mistakes.

In Japan, there is a common expression, "Every thief has his reasons." The expression applies directly to our own actions. Even if a mistake is obvious to others, the person who made it will usually have some way to justify it and avoid accountability.

"I haven't done anything wrong. I've made the right decision. I'm just misunderstood." It's only natural to think this way. So many of us make excuses and try to justify themselves.

But how do others perceive us when they hear these excuses? Think about how you feel when you hear others make excuses and you'll quickly understand. Excuses only make matters worse. Everyone knows this deep inside, but it's human nature to serve them up anyway.

The greater problem, in truth, may be using these excuses to lie to ourselves. That sort of poor decision-making circle is not only pointless but dangerous. The best response to failure is to reflect upon why you failed and take steps to ensure you don't fail in the same way again. When you attempt to justify your actions, you lose sight of the real reasons for your failure. With the real reasons not allowed to surface, you won't be able to develop the right countermeasures.

The decision-making death spiral only gets worse the longer it continues. In fact, I must admit to deceiving myself on more than a few occasions. When I'm not paying attention, even for just a moment, I catch myself trying to justify my mistakes. I can't help it. But experience has taught me to seek out a personal workaround.

That's why I find others to play catch with and make a conscious effort to expose myself to opinions I might not like. If you always have to be right, you are actually creating limits for yourself. That's why I so often recommend that you should always start by questioning yourself. And the first question should be: Am I rationalizing my behavior? The answer may be yes.

22 Interrogate your intuition with hard numbers

Intuition is just the first step of any great idea. After that, bring on the numbers.

For example, let's say you get an idea: "If I opened a bookstore in front of the train station, it would probably do well." That's just your intuition talking.

Many have succeeded in business relying on intuition alone, but everyone forgets something more important: A lot more have failed *because of* intuition. If everyone succeeded on intuition, it would hardly be something to boast about.

I'm not saying intuition itself is bad or always wrong. Rather, intuition should be viewed as a rough sketch—a first draft of an idea with more details to come. Hard numbers and metrics that can serve as guideposts are essential if we are to monitor our intuition. It's the combination of intuition and numbers that generates new ideas and pivot points. In business, adding details and metrics to intuition can clearly reveal obstacles ahead. Or, conversely, sometimes they generate important milestones that will lead a project forward. Many a great idea will fail when intuition is embraced without details. Interrogate your intuition to give your rough draft the details it needs.

For example, let's say your intuition tells you a particular location near your train station would be perfect for a new bookstore. Interrogate your intuition that the bookstore would do well by looking at specific figures. Research how many potential customers walk past the station every day, the level of sales at nearby local stores, and the foot traffic at bookstores at the next station over. Consider margins, rents, personnel costs and other data, and, based on all of that, calculate your projected level of profit.

Once you've filled in the details of your plan, step back from it and look at the big picture. Having examined the detailed figures, you should expose it to your intuitive mind again. Every time you do this, you will develop an elevated sense of what is taking place each day in front of the station.

Usually, when you examine the numbers, the result is going to be lower than what you initially guessed. We all tend to be overly optimistic. Usually there's a good reason why there's not a bookstore in front of the station already. If your quick calculations revealed that a profit could be made, then some opportunist would have jumped at the chance before you.

Now, this doesn't mean you should give up. Take your detailed plan, consider the big picture you just framed out, and drill down on ways to bring the numbers that were surprisingly low closer to your initial expectations. Are there any gaps in your projections? How could you achieve even better numbers? New ideas will flow and be even more powerful than the first one. This is your second wave of intuition and it is bolstered by your now more refined metrics. It should be more specific than the rough sketch you started with since now you understand the ins and outs of operating a bookstore. In other words, your business model will be clearer.

Now put this new model into numbers once again. The numbers you need will probably be different. Turn your intuition into numbers and go for an even deeper, more informed level of intuition. Then turn that into numbers. By repeating this process, you'll build a robust business model, rooted in reality.

This is the only way to make the correct use of intuition. You should value personal intuition, but you can't develop a business by relying on intuition alone. Bolster it with numbers and see the true value of your big idea.

23 Aim to understand the framework

Every building has an underlying structural frame that keeps it standing. And even the architect who wants to build the most beautiful building in the world must have an understanding of that frame.

The Japanese are fond of dividing the world into two camps: professionals versus amateurs. The professionals are quick to dismiss the amateurs not simply because they lack specialized knowledge. After all, skills can always be obtained through education. Professionals will argue it is more than skills; it is additionally the element of framework. Professionals embrace a mental framework of their field and they use it to engage in analytical decision making.

In marketing, there is a pattern of thought that often leads to superior results. It's not so unlike the patterns of moves that play out in *shogi*, or Japanese chess. These patterns are not based on common sense. They might resemble common sense in some ways, but they're actually more strategic than meets the unskilled player's eye. Even when the experts make seemingly irrational moves, a strategic pattern is likely to be driving their decision.

The reason some aspiring professionals have accumulated a lot of specialized knowledge but have not become experts straddles this fine mental line. The pro sees patterns that the amateur cannot yet analyze and interpret.

Conversely, as long as you have the framework clear in your head, even if you are missing some of the specialized knowledge, you can still understand the big picture. In business, being able to understand the big picture is mission critical. Rather than dive into all the most minute, technical aspects of a problem, first make efforts to understand the overall framework to analyze it properly. You might understand marketing but not human resources. You might understand operations, but not technology. You might be able to read a blueprint, but not be able to make heads or tails of an accounting ledger. None of us can be experts in everything. The larger the company, the more specialized each employee becomes. You often hear colleagues admit they don't understand what goes on in the department next door. When departments become siloes, this gets even worse.

The reason work is divided up is to boost overall efficiency. It's not done to discourage collaboration and innovation. In truth, highly specialized groups within an organization can only work effectively if they come together organically and work across company siloes. In practice, there's no job that can be fully completed by one specialized area. Understanding the framework of another field is extremely useful when drawing up project plans or trying to come up with new ideas, if only as a form of reference. Knowing the framework of another core skillset will help you understand the essence of why a success is achieved. You might also be able to apply that thinking to your own work.

Don't focus just on understanding the framework of your own field, but also be curious about those other fields and study those, too. This will add to the resources you have to draw on and the more of these you have, the better. The more resources you have, the more open you will become to new ways of thinking. And in turn, this will ultimately enrich your capacity to think creatively in your own specialized area.

24 Create solutions that break down barriers and reveal new challenges

There are very few problems in business that cannot be solved. I've always found that something can be done, even in the most challenging of situations.

Of course, if you're up against the forces of nature, some things simply cannot be changed for the better. For example, none of us can stop an earthquake from happening using current science and technology. But we can certainly construct buildings (even entire cities), dams and roads, and other infrastructure that can withstand major earthquakes. Skyscrapers in Tokyo, for example, can withstand earthquakes of level 6 on the Japanese seismic intensity scale, a level that will knock over older wooden buildings. How prepared we are for earthquakes is a decision that we make as a society. Society is created by humans, so humans can also change it.

Likewise, business is a construct of society. Unlike instances in which we battle the forces of Mother Nature (and can only prepare to withstand them), most business problems can be solved through creativity and innovation. Nothing is outside the realm *of the possible.*

What I find fascinating is that just as soon as you have applied your best creativity and technological innovation to solve a problem, you inevitably run into a completely new problem on the horizon soon after. Solving one problem only redirects you to the next one to tackle in the future.

If you're now thinking, "In that case, why bother solving any problems at all?" then unfortunately I might add that you're probably not cut out for the world of business. Ultimately, business is simply a never-ending series of creative problem solving.

In Greek mythology, Sisyphus was made to push a boulder up a hill as a punishment. Just before he reached the top, the boulder would cruelly roll away from him, down to the bottom of the hill. He then had to keep on pushing this boulder up the hill for all eternity. Although business is similar to this in so many ways, there's one fundamental difference. The problem that awaits you at the top of the hill is a completely new problem—one that you haven't seen before. And this new problem is always more complex than the one you just solved. So, unlike Sisyphus, you're not repeatedly climbing up the same hill. Rather, you're rising to new heights. And as the problems become more complex, the more you will grow by solving them. By scaling even higher mountains, you are able to come face to face with even stiffer challenges. Always continuing the climb is the absolute essence of business success.

Some might ask where the excitement lies in this process, and I can only reply that grappling with problems is the most exciting part of what we do in business. After resolving one problem with all your creative resources, an even more complex challenge comes into view. Your fighting spirit must rise up again to the new challenge before you. Some might see this as punishment, but the personal satisfaction of success far outweighs any short-term pain, based on my own personal experiences.

25 Identify your weaknesses. Fix them or find workarounds

Business strategy and sport have a lot in common, but one key point of difference is that in business it can make sense to admit your weaknesses.

When exceptional tennis players don't feel 100 percent physically, they will probably try to keep it quiet. Disclosure of an injury might allow an opponent to attack a weakness. For this reason, they often won't discuss injuries before a big competition. They simply alter their training methods to both heal and prepare at the same time.

But business is different. In business, you can have as many personal weak point or faults as you like, because you can overcome them. Making up for them involves recognizing them first and taking countermeasures. Only a failure to acknowledge your weak points leads to disaster.

This is why it is essential to listen to things we don't want to hear.

If this was a one-on-one competition, our faults and weaknesses would be painfully obvious. In business, however, our personal shortcomings are not always visible. So many different factors determine whether you win or lose. Capital resources and the unique talents and abilities of colleagues all play a part. The playing field is never level. That's why it is such a challenge to identify solutions when you run into a rough patch. And every business, large or small, has a few along the way.

But there's one bit of solace you can take during a rough patch: No one is good at everything. Everyone has weak points. Everyone has flaws. And, if you eliminate your flaws, your performance will improve. That's why it's crucial to understand precisely where your own flaws lie. Don't let your ego interfere with personal introspection. Be humble and make sure you understand your own flaws first.

Once you have, decide if you can overcome the deficit by learning a new skill or if your weakness can be quickly overcome by reaching out to a mentor, colleague, or outside resource. There are many ways to go about it: Develop a network of personal advisors to address the gap, or invite others to come and work with you directly.

An empowering first step, if you have time, is to learn something yourself. For example, if you feel communicating in another language is indispensable to your company's success, obviously the best path is to master the language yourself. That said, you need to be flexible as well, because in the end, you need to balance learning with on-the-job results. Of course, sometimes it will be more efficient to hire an interpreter with perfect language skills than to invest time to learn a new language. You should carefully weigh the time required against the potential results.

Making this personal assessment is surprisingly difficult. Many of us will skirt the issue, without making that judgment, and without taking that hard, objective look at ourselves. Once you understand your shortcomings, the decision to overcome any personal deficiency is much easier. If you can wedge a personal time slot into your day for learning, then the self-study option makes the most sense. But if time and opportunity cost make that impossible, then the best alternative is to reach out to your network as soon as you can and develop a game plan that leverages the talents of others.

The key is not to let rivals put any additional ground between you and them. Always work to close the gap and eliminate any weakness that is holding you back.

26 Never let your mental energy levels drop

Whenever you engage in work, challenge yourself to maintain a high level of mental energy at all times. This isn't always easy, but actively reinvigorating mental energy and motivation is an essential part of peak work performance. Sometimes we don't even realize it, especially when stress and overload trick us into believing we are being productive when in actuality we are not. You must constantly find ways to recharge and boost your own internal batteries.

There are all kinds of methods to boost motivation. For instance, I've heard that before he begins filming, Steven Spielberg always watches Akira Kurosawa's *Seven Samurai*. This is his way of boosting his motivation. They say the first time he saw the film, he felt that it represented the purest form of cinema he'd ever seen. Watching it probably brings back his memories of how moved he was by that first viewing. Being inspired by others often boosts your mental energy levels. At such times, your brain can achieve greater levels of creativity and engagement to problem-solve and execute an idea.

For me, it's exercise. I regularly go to the gym. I work up a sweat over 90 minutes, two to three times a week. First I use the sauna and get my heart rate up. Then I do a half-hour of cardio followed by various kinds of strength training. My exercise routine gets my entire body working at peak levels, removes stress, and both relaxes and stimulates my mind by the time I hit the showers.

Exercise in itself is a good energizer but, more than that, it reminds me of how I felt when I was a young boy crazy about tennis, dreaming about becoming a professional player.

When you're a child, the smallest things are exciting because you are dreaming about them without conscious effort. But somehow when you become an adult, you find yourself less easily moved, and it becomes harder to drum up that same level of excitement. You must approach each working day with this level of enthusiasm and engagement. If mental fatigue is dragging you down, then a day off to recharge may be worth it.

You don't want your own depleted energy levels to rub off on your team. It affects the morale of the whole team, and can lead to failures and mistakes. More than anything, when this happens, work stops being fun. When you stop enjoying your work, it becomes just a routine. At that point, you will lose your ability to make well-thought-out decisions or creatively think outside the box.

Keep your energy levels high, and try to always maintain a positive attitude toward your work.

Know that continuing to work without sufficient mental energy will only lead to failure.

3

The Value of Relationships

As the famous expression goes: keep your friends close and your enemies closer. And when I say *enemies,* I don't mean true outside antagonists. I'm talking about rivals—perhaps those within your own company. How well do you relate to others? How well do you understand the theory of relationships? Friend or foe, understanding what makes a relationship productive is essential.

27 Offer value–added services. Anything less is meaningless

In everything from your products to your work effort, always offer value.

Understanding value is the key to success in business. Imagine two watches in a glass case before you. One is a $50 watch, the other is a $10,000 watch. As you gaze through the glass, can you tell the difference?

After quartz watches were invented, the price of a watch ceased to bear any relation to its ability to accurately keep time. A $50 watch tells the same time as a $10,000 watch. So why would someone pay a premium price for a watch? The only reason is the additional value that you would perceive in wearing the more expensive watch.

Every product or service faces the same test when offered to the consumer, not just watches. Everyone in business must constantly be asking whether what they provide, in terms of products or services, has an added value above and beyond the price. Creating a product that a consumer can substitute with another is unacceptable. Brands must matter to sustain long-term growth.

Do you know the true source of your profit margin—why customers are buying what you sell? What is it that distinguishes your product or service above all others? Does your customer actually feel a level of satisfaction above the actual price of the product? And what can you do to increase that satisfaction—whether it be convenience, functionality, or celebrity glamor? Continuing to think about this is the best way to develop your business. It's a question you must revisit again and again over time.

If you're ambitious and you want to excel as an employee and as a leader, it's also useful to ask yourself what skills and expertise are adding value in your personal interactions with colleagues, teams, and customers. The product of your work and your work habits, after all, are a service. That service also needs to carry added value. Why does your company pay you? If you think that it's only because you've signed a contract, then you are not going to achieve all that is possible for yourself. Strive to boost what makes you valuable to your colleagues. Committing to this process isn't hard. All it takes is a little time and effort.

I'm sure everyone who leads a team knows this, but if you carefully analyze the difference between direct reports who are outstanding and those who aren't, you'll realize that it's only slight. Even so, slight differences translate into additional perceived value for leaders whose performance depends on efficient execution of ideas. This is because most people don't make that extra small effort. Every effort in business counts. Those who surprise because of attention to small details will find it creates enormous opportunities for personal growth. Incrementally, it can lead to big wins for organizations and leaders that foster this initiative at an individual level.

What's your added value? Think hard about it and try to do something concrete to increase it, however small. That small effort may be the difference between success and failure. Always remember that a service that does not add value is meaningless.

28 Put yourself in their shoes

To transform the world, start by seeing another person's perspective. This is a lesson I learned early. But it did not come naturally to me; I needed to be taught.

When I was a child, I had a tendency to do my own thing. In my early years in school, I often had to stand in the corner for disobeying the rules. I was not bothered much by this, but I remember my older sister was upset when her classmates teased her about my misbehavior.

It was my grandmother who taught me my lesson in empathy. She could see that I was not considering others when I acted. I used to love to visit my grandmother in her store and watch her as she engaged with her customers, selling tobacco or ice cream. It's important, she told me, to think about how others are feeling. Put yourself in their shoes.

It's a lesson that had an enormous impact on me, and has stuck with me ever since. After all, it's a fundamental principle of religions and moral systems around the world. You could perhaps even say that all moral codes are just variations on this idea expressed in different ways.

Seeing the world from another's perspective is transformational for both sides. If people actually did this, virtually all the world's problems—war, famine, the North-South divide, ethnic conflict, even environmental problems—could readily be solved. Conversely, it's precisely because we don't take this moral code to heart that the world is experiencing so many major problems.

The ability to see a situation from someone else's perspective is unique to humankind. It's a definitive sign of our common humanity, more so than the ability to use tools or build a fire. People aren't born with this ability, because it's not inherited genetically. It's shared with us. It is culturally acquired each time a community of humans aspires to perpetuate what they all hold sacred.

The reason I was so struck by my grandmother's words is probably because I was too young to have ever considered perspectives other than my own before. Today, that lesson rings true for me every day as I work to consider the perspectives of my customers, my colleagues, my investors, and my family. This lesson she taught me as I sat in her store is with me as I travel the world, running a global business.

Think of it this way: If you don't understand another person's perspective, it will be nearly impossible to have them accept your own. Of course, if you're in a far superior position to the person you're talking to, you can impose your views.

But making an executive decision isn't as valuable as having the individual understand the decision from your point of view. And, in the long run, imposing on others will hurt you in ways you cannot anticipate. The expression, "What goes around, comes around," cannot be more true.

It is particularly important in business to think long and hard about this dynamic between you and others. In simple terms, in business, if you make a profit, someone else may face an equivalent loss. A key point that leads to success in business is how well you can reconcile these opposing interests. It is only when those opposing interests align that you will be able to create an ongoing relationship. To achieve this, you must think about things from the perspective of the other stakeholder.

To be clear, I'm not in favor of bending too far. Seeing a business deal as a winning proposition means that you have explored the transaction from both sides. It's about finding the point where you are able to generate profit and the other party is also gaining a sufficient profit. Whether you're selling something, offering a service, or involved in a major deal, you'll never fail if you negotiate in this way.

The most successful business deals happen when you align the deal from the vantage point of someone else, while remaining keenly aware of your own.

29 See the essence of things

Why do people buy things? When you can understand the real reasons (and they may be hard to see at first), you have a clear advantage.

When we started Rakuten Ichiba in Japan, every other internet shopping mall out there had already failed. The prevailing public opinion was that this was tangible proof that internet shopping malls would never work. I had my reasons for thinking otherwise.

I thought about the must-have functionality of internet shopping malls, what their unique advantages would be, and what the gaps in the online experience were. I thought through every possible aspect of internet shopping malls. And my analysis lead to one conclusion: If you could fully leverage the unique advantages of the internet, you could create a shopping mall with a merchandise offering and competitive prices far superior to brick-and-mortar stores. And if you could create a system that provided customers with real-time information on products and prices, success would be a given. Needless to say, this was the cornerstone for Rakuten Ichiba. If I'd given up on the idea just because other people said it was impossible, Rakuten would never have come into existence.

It's essential in the real world of business to ask the simple question why, and to continue asking questions that allow you to peel away the layers until you can see the true nature of things. Now that Rakuten Ichiba has taken off and continued to grow over the last 20 years, I have never stopped asking the questions that created success.

So why do we buy things in the first place? While we can talk about people "buying things," there are so many different kinds of "shopping." You could say we buy what's necessary, but is that really true? Is that all there is to it? Do we really only buy things out of necessity?

This is something I thought about a lot in those days—whether I was asleep, awake, watching TV, walking around town or at work. I always had this question somewhere bouncing around in my brain.

We all buy things for various reasons but all these reasons fundamentally have one thing in common: it's enjoyable. In other words, shopping is entertainment. That core idea underlies everything we do at Rakuten Ichiba. It prompts millions of customers to visit our site every day.

Seeing the essence of things isn't just the job of philosophers. It's even more important in business to determine the true nature of things. Every employee must have that level of attention to detail. If you only pay attention to the latest superficial trends, you'll never really come up with a revolutionary idea. Great business ideas and directions are born from looking into the essence of things. Steve Jobs is famously credited with understanding that design was just as important as functionality when it came to creating great technology products. His design aesthetic is closely bound up in the Apple brand—in everything from the décor of its stores to the design of the iPhone. He understood the essence of what motivated his customers—and why they came back again and again.

When you hit a roadblock, go back to the essence. Look into it deeply. Why did you end up here? Keep asking why—that simple question—in order to work your way back to the essence. That's where you start out again to search for a real solution.

You can't solve anything without a clear picture of what makes a product, service, or experience invaluable to the consumer. When you work backward to uncover original insights—the essence of things—you can discover the ideas that will drive a company forward.

30 Size up risk by quantifying it

Risk is a word we so often associate with the pairing *risk avoidance*. So much so that most feel it's prudent to simply steer clear of risk overall. But I would argue there is another way to see risk. Consider this: the Japanese word for "crisis" is composed of two characters: the one for "danger" and the character for "opportunity." Within the concept of risk there is certainly a warning, but also a path forward, for those willing to make the effort and face the possible dangers.

Successful business leaders know they must face risk to succeed. Daring to face risk head-on leads to success in business. If you look back in history, you'll find countless examples of successful companies that were risk-takers. Bill Gates dropped out of Harvard after two years to found Microsoft. The Wright Brothers invested years in their pursuit of flight. That trend continues today with individuals such as Elon Musk exploring the possibilities of business in space and autonomous driving. I am on a mission to cure cancer and I've helped to found a medical startup to do just that. No business leaders, myself included, are ever presented with a sure thing. All of us have to embrace risk.

When we started out with Rakuten Ichiba, we were ourselves risk-takers. At that time, the idea of an internet shopping mall was already regarded in Japan as a business model that clearly didn't work. More than one pundit suggested we were more likely to fail than succeed. But we took that risk nonetheless.

Some might call taking a risk like this, or rather, betting against popular wisdom, to be a form of gambling. Undeniably, business includes gambling-like elements. But I would argue that the essentials of business are completely different from gambling.

I did bet against a risk. But I did so only after quantifying the size and type of risk I faced, reducing it as much as I could, and preparing ways to mitigate it. It wasn't an all-or-nothing bet that would be simply won or lost.

The biggest single risk I faced at that time was the possibility that the internet wouldn't spread as fast as I'd predicted. However appealing we made Rakuten Ichiba, with the level of internet penetration that existed in 1997, it appeared to many that our idea was never going to reach a mass audience. The business model depended on a projection that internet use would rise quickly. Rakuten Ichiba could have gone bankrupt if widespread adoption of the internet did not play out as we anticipated.

To minimize this risk, we set the monthly fee for operating a store on Rakuten Ichiba at a low ¥50,000, or about US$400, an almost crazy price for the times, and asked store owners to pay six months in advance. Even if internet use didn't rise as quickly as we projected, the fee assured we'd be able to maintain a minimum cash flow to keep the business afloat. We kept capital and employee numbers low. We believed the smaller we were, the longer we'd be able to wait for internet use to pick up. We didn't just take a risk, but also tried to estimate how long we could afford to pursue this opportunity. We determined the type and the size of the risk and prepared as best we could to deal with it over a variety of scenarios.

Risk-taking leads to opportunities because those very fields with high risks often can be disputed by those prepared to challenge the status quo. Rakuten Ichiba effectively had no competitors in Japan at the outset, which gave us just the window of opportunity we needed. Needless to say, this contributed significantly to its success.

If you understand clearly the type and size of the risk you face, and come up with robust plans to deal with it, great risks will become great opportunities.

31 Seek out best practices all around you

In your work, first look for inspiration close at hand. Do the same when you hit a roadblock. The person sitting right next to you might be able to help you through it.

Strangely enough, we often forget to draw upon what lies around us. Like the characters in the children's play *The Blue Bird*, we like to look for answers far away, believing the far away solutions are the most valuable. This is an illusion. We figure intuitively that the harder something is to obtain, the more valuable it must be. This may be so with precious metals and gemstones, but not when it comes to getting your work done efficiently.

The wheel does not need to be reinvented everywhere. Our workspaces in Japan and Germany may not look exactly the same, but the essence of the underlying work in those locations does not change all that much. The problem-solving in each location may be remarkably similar and easily duplicated, once colleagues share information and strategy.

In teams at Rakuten, for example, we often combine colleagues who can solve a particular problem with others who can't. That way, the ability to learn that particular problem solving skill is close at hand. The curious and engaged mind will learn and excel. Those who don't see this as an opportunity really aren't looking. Those who reach out to colleagues to understand how they excel at getting their jobs done are destined themselves for greater success.

Let me share something here. At Rakuten Ichiba, we started up a system known as "two-minute calls." The system was that the person in charge must call clients on the phone within two minutes of receiving an email request for information. The potential clients who receive a phone call before they've even had time to close the Rakuten page where they made a request, as you'd expect, are sometimes a little surprised, but this also works to build customer trust. And customers appreciate that the rapid response isn't facilitated by a computer program alone, but is fully supported by customer services representatives who follow up.

This system increases the likelihood that the person requesting materials will go to the next stage, of signing a contract or engaging with us, and it has been extremely effective for Rakuten Ichiba. I call it a system, but actually, it's not all that complicated. All we did was designate someone to call the customers sending us emails for information within two minutes of receiving them.

Later, we applied this principle to respond to customers posting negative ratings on Ichiba as well. We were keen to get to the bottom of issues quickly, and we also wanted to let customers know that we were paying attention to their feedback.

While you can see that this system follow-up could have applications in various internet businesses, it took a considerable length of time to spread within the Rakuten Group. The colleagues closest to us didn't notice how effective and easy this system was to implement. At the same time, however, the system spread rapidly through our US subsidiaries. This is not to say that our American teams are better than our Japanese teams, but rather, that the Rakuten employees here in Japan couldn't see what was right under their noses, while our staff on the other side of the Pacific could.

Success can be that close without being seen. Every job done well often comes down to execution and operation. We need to recognize that outstanding talent within our organizations and ask others to adopt their best practice methods of execution and operation. You can't copy talent, but anyone can imitate best practices in execution and operation.

32 Listen especially closely to people you disagree with

Everyone gladly listens to opinions that make them feel good. But it's the opinions that make you feel uncomfortable or perhaps even angry that deserve your greatest attention. It's not just that you may not be mentally prepared to hear such opinions, but also because the older you get, the less you will find others are willing to say such things directly to your face.

It's better when you first enter the workforce. You're pelted with negative opinions from every side. You have to clench your teeth and hear them out. You might be blamed for something you didn't do, or know that the opinion is based on a misunderstanding. You may sometimes even experience criticism that seems malicious. But it's best just to take it all in, and think of it as a form of trial-by-fire training. This might not be the best choice of words, but as I said above, "Every thief has his reasons." Even someone doing the wrong thing has reasons for their actions. Every opinion is likely to have at least one takeaway that you'll find useful. Take the time when you're alone to write down suggestions, even from your harshest critics, in a notebook and use them to better yourself. This is the best way of turning the tables on those who criticize you without constructive purpose. After all, getting angry rarely solves any problems.

While criticism may sting, real problems arise when you stop listening to others. When this starts to occur, you must be sure to convey through your attitude and words that you want to hear all opinions, no matter how difficult they may be to hear. That's why I don't have a door on my office. I want everyone to feel free to come to me with strong opinions and objections whenever they like.

I also always say, "If you have an opinion, please share it with me. I might sometimes react with anger, since I'm only human. But no matter how angry I get, no matter how much I dislike hearing it, I guarantee I will never mark you down for it, so don't hold back!"

I hesitate to say this, but to be honest, not every opinion I hear is valid and valuable. While they may not be wrong, some of the opinions I encounter can often be short-sighted or miss the mark. It's not that the individual failed to deliver the opinion constructively or that the opinion lacks depths. More often than not, the opinion lacks perspective. Management tends to see things from more of a big-picture perspective than individual employees typically do. Without this kind of bird's-eye view, it's impossible to choose the best path. That's why, I have to admit, I do feel that many of the opinions I hear miss the mark. But if I actually said this to everyone who is brave enough to share ideas, I'd end up like the fabled emperor with his new clothes. And while this is a scary thought, what's even more terrifying is the prospect of those around the emperor ceasing to think for themselves.

An environment in which there can be no debate is lethal to a person's spirit and powers of judgment. To avoid this danger of too much group-speak, you must always be very conscious to keep an independent and open mind. There may be only one worthwhile opinion among every hundred. But even so, that opinion might hit on a serious mistake you've made. That single opinion can save a whole company. When industrial innovation firm 3M had a glue experiment go wrong, someone saw the potential of the non-drying, failed adhesive—and the Post-It note was created.

Not only that, but the leader who refuses to listen can never create an open, communicative environment in which every member of the organization will take the initiative to think through things. This is extremely important for any organization.

Be particularly respectful of the opinions of those with different values from your own, and demonstrate this respect through your constructive actions. As an example from my own work, as Rakuten has grown and we have moved to new office space, I have transitioned from a traditional office with walls and a door to an open floor plan in which my office is simply a corner of the large space. Anyone can see me, approach me, or talk to me. There are no walls to come between us. This has many positive aspects, but the one I point out here is the opportunity for opinion sharing. I am always visible and I believe this makes others see me as more accessible, so they are more likely to approach me and share their ideas.

33 Value the balance between cooperation and competition

Just as in the natural world, in any organization there must be both cooperation and competition. If there's only cooperation, you lose your sense of urgency. If there's only competition, teamwork becomes messy or simply stops.

It's often noted that Rakuten is a very competitive company. But it's also a place where everyone is encouraged to share a sense of accomplishment about their work. Employees are rivals, but also irreplaceable teammates. This might seem like a paradox, but it's not at Rakuten.

This isn't just the case for individual organizations. It's also the case for society as a whole. The business world is becoming more and more complicated, and countless areas have arisen where you have to cooperate with your rivals. I've even heard there's a word for this in English—*coopetition*—to mean a relationship where you are both cooperating and competing. Coopetition is the act of cooperation between competing companies. Certain businesses gain an advantage by using a judicious mixture of cooperation with supplier, customers and firms producing complementary or related products. For example, Ford and Toyota teamed up in 2013 to design new hybrid systems technology, Microsoft and Intel created a long working relationship around Intel chips and Microsoft software, and the US Postal Service entered into coopetition arrangements with rivals FedEx and UPS.

It's important that cooperation and competition exist side-by-side, and that they are well-balanced. To strike this balance, you must abandon any law-of-the-jungle ideas you may have and look at your business from a broader perspective. You must realize that without the development of society or an industry, individuals and businesses alone are not able to develop.

Competition is important, but does it contribute to overall development or hinder it? You have to pause for a second sometimes and really think about this. Should you be competing or cooperating? Swallow your pride and think about it objectively from a third person's perspective. When you should cooperate, put your heart into it. When it's time to compete, make every effort, but always compete fairly. This is the best approach, both for companies and for individuals.

34 Teaching others will help you grow

A leader must always be a teacher. It is the best way to lead and the best way to learn.

No doubt, many of us may feel burdened at first when asked to guide junior team members. But which of us haven't benefited from a colleague willing to share invaluable insights earned from their own experiences? Successful people must learn that teaching is part of the leader's job and what's more, both mentor and mentee benefit from it.

To teach someone something, you must think about and analyze things you normally do unconsciously and put them into words in a way that others can understand. Teaching would be easy if work processes and methods were always exactly the same. However, in actual work there are always special circumstances, and you often run into situations that can't be predicted. So you have to be flexible and change processes and methods in response. You probably won't be able to teach this kind of flexibility if you don't always think deeply about how you judge situations and deal with things. Teaching is not a burden when you reflect on the insights you might also receive from those you mentor.

Of course, it's easy to get lost in the daily pressures of work. Few of us think that deeply about our jobs. That's exactly why guiding junior team members will lead to improvement in your own performance.

From time to time, I meet people who are exceptional teachers. They may not stand out in the business world, but I'm sure all of us can recall instances of great instruction, either in the classroom or on the playing field. Great sports coaches make an excellent example of this experience. Great coaches have worked incredibly hard early on in life. They're skilled teachers because they've thought deeply about their sport, repeating every possible kind of trial and error. One Japanese precept applies here: "Experience hardship early, even if it costs you."

Teaching others can be a way you yourself learn new skills. The people you are teaching will have different abilities and personalities. With some, positive encouragement is fine, while others need to be scolded. Teaching others will therefore also help you develop a discerning eye for people with talent and potential.

One more thing: If you are going to guide others, you have to make sure you can do your own job properly first. One often hears of young new employees who lack professionalism when they joined a company, but as soon as the next wave of new employees joined, they suddenly develop the skills they need to excel. It's also sometimes said that children raise their parents. I've seen this with my own eyes. Young team members often have much to share with their leaders.

You must not neglect teaching, as it will improve your own performance as well.

35 Develop win–win relationships

Aligning opposing interests is a fundamental principle of business.

In days gone by, it's been said that pirates were also traders. They often wore two hats, depending on whom they were dealing with on any given day. In other words, whether they would plunder or trade in any given situation depended on which was more efficient or profitable. Even plundering has its costs.

This is an extreme example I've raised to emphasize my point. But I'm sure most of us can draw parallel stories from modern experience. Logic dictates that trading partners will have opposing interests. A one-yen profit for the seller is a one-yen loss for the buyer. You don't have to be a pirate to want to take up an opportunity to make that profit. But there are good reasons why you won't be able to build a business to scale in this way.

There was a time when piracy was rampant (it still is in some places). But when the world became "smaller," pirates lost their place in it. I suspect this change was due more to the increasing importance of trust in business transactions than to crackdowns on piracy. Trading simply became more profitable than plundering.

The internet has further shrunk the world. And it has made relationships based on trust more important than ever to business. Building relationships based on trust is essential to growth, not only with customers and business partners but with society at large as well.

To develop relationships based on trust, you must align opposing interests, something that might seem to go against profit-motivated logic. But win-win relationships need not be counter to profit. Thinking this way simply means ensuring parties on both sides of the transaction benefit.

Here's an example from my own business. I founded Rakuten to be an online marketplace, and to make that happen, I needed merchants to use my site as their online host. Since I was brand new, I could not hope to attract big merchants to my marketplace and so I turned my focus to small and mid-sized merchants. At first, they were not that easy to sign up, either. Many of them were wary about investing in something as new as an online marketplace. To overcome this hesitancy, I had to create win-win situations. My early sales staff and I looked for ways to build relationships with our clients. Often, in those early days, we went with our clients to purchase their first computer and help them set up. As we grew, we sought to provide our merchants with the tools they needed to succeed. And we did not overmanage them and create a lot of rules about how they had to run their businesses online. We trusted them to do what was necessary to be successful on our platform. We didn't want to give up profits, and neither did they. So we created situations in which we could both be profitable. That became the foundation of our company.

What makes this logic-defying feat possible is the creation of value. If the transaction generates new value, both you and the other party will benefit. The difficult thing is that you must constantly generate that additional value. As soon as a company loses its ability to add value, its social mission ends. An entity that only exploits society is destined to go the way of the pirates.

This, of course, also applies to us at Rakuten. We all must keep on striving to ensure the generation of new value. We must constantly be thinking hard about what we can do to help our customers lead richer lives and about how we can contribute to society as an organization—and ensure that we are delivering on that. Not only should this be the core mission of anyone in business today, it is also the best way to beat the competition.

36 Start with good footwork
Speed and agility are winning behaviors.

Being light on your feet is an essential quality for anyone in business. All the outstanding businesspeople I've ever met have had the ability to act quickly. I can't think of a single exception. They make decisions quickly, moving swiftly to implement ideas into action, without delay. They complete even small tasks with all due speed. And that goes even more for difficult tasks or those others would rather keep putting off. In other words, they will take care of the things that others will postpone indefinitely. Many of them are also impatient, but I assume that's because they know instinctively that it's also the most efficient way to be. Without knowing that, you will never be a success in business.

It is a common misconception that success in business is governed by an individual's innate ability. While we all have different levels of ability, most of us would also accept that those with superior skills and intellects don't necessarily become outstanding business people.

However, when it comes to being agile, there are no exceptions. If you compare those who do what they can today with those who put things off until tomorrow, you'll find the former are always the outstanding business people. In other words, being light-footed is even more of a defining factor than brains. This is because, far more than a difference in skill levels, time is of the essence in business.

A day lasts 24 hours, a year 365 days. Time is a level playing field. How efficiently we use that equally allotted time is what will set us apart. Those who are quick on their feet will use their time many times more efficiently than those who are not. It's the equivalent of being given that much more time to work with. In that sense, time is relative in business. No matter how skilled you are, if you're only fitting 24 hours into a day, you'll never beat someone who fits in the equivalent of 30 or 40 hours.

If you're quick enough, you can overtake those who are more skilled. In other words, being light on your feet is an important business skill in itself. Also, in contrast to other skills, there are no limits to how much you can improve through your own commitment.

If you decide to do something, do it now. Don't put it off. View procrastination as the equivalent of doing nothing. In other words, decide then and there whether or not to do something. If you do this, work won't pile up. As a result, you'll always be able to put all of your energy into the challenges facing you.

Many business publications noted that Rakuten moved quickly to purchase the voice and messaging app Viber in February 2014 for $900 million. Later in the same month, Facebook purchased WhatsApp, another messaging app, for around $22 billion. Many speculated that our purchase price might have been considerably inflated if we had taken just a few weeks longer to close the deal.

Of course, you don't have to immediately decide everything right now. Just remember always to be light on your feet. You might not always keep to it. Sometimes it will be better not to rush a decision but to wait. But you must always be sure to make that assessment. In principle, you should never procrastinate, but there are times when holding off will be the better option. That may seem paradoxical, but it's one more thing to keep in mind as you aim to become light-footed. As an example from my own history, when I was a young man and I left my job at the Industrial Bank of Japan to start a business, I did not jump into it right away. I took time to research my next step, ask advice of my mentors, and look for the best opportunity. If I'd succumbed to the pressure to start my new business quickly, I might've chosen an industry other than e-commerce and internet services. (In fact, I was seriously considering a business in craft beer.) But because I knew better than to rush, I gathered all my information before I made a decision. The trick is to understand the line between good preparation and procrastination.

37 Report, contact, and consult

In Japan, these three words are considered the 1-2-3 of doing business. We are very familiar with this recommended cycle of actions. But while we all know the principle, it is much more difficult to act on it all of the time. A huge proportion of business blunders could have been averted just by upholding this principle, yet the failure to observe this principle is apparent everywhere in companies, from new employees to the most senior in the organization. Consider how VW might have handled its issues around emissions testing, or Samsung might have headed off problems with its batteries, if everyone in those companies had been communicating appropriately.

Understanding the communications principles is a key step to success:

- ◆ *Report* refers to communicating results, or "this is what happened."
- ◆ *Contact* means keeping others informed along the way, or "this is what's happening."
- ◆ *Consult* refers to looking for advice in advance of taking action, or "I'd like to do this—what do you think?"

This is not to say we must always report, contact, and consult about absolutely everything. Doing that would make us all robots. What companies really need are confident, analytical people who can act based on their own judgment. If you always reported, contacted, and consulted about absolutely everything, you'd undoubtedly be making a nuisance of yourself with your manager.

The key here is your judgment on which items require consultation in advance, which require ongoing contact, and which will be fine with a report on completion. The basic principle should be that the degree of importance of the task will guide your judgment, but, in addition to that, your relationship with your management and your own abilities will also be important factors. So this is something you must think through yourself. You must think carefully about how each task requires reporting, contacting, or consultation—and from the perspective of your management. If you're not thinking soundly and with proper judgment, you'll start to confuse reports, contacts, and consultation and end up making work more difficult. You'll end up being shouted at for not consulting in advance on one task, and then told off for seeking advice about trivial matters on the next one.

The one thing I'd like you to remember is that just about everything will go more smoothly if you continue to report on your work. This becomes even more important as you move up the career ladder and take on a higher level of responsibility. It's crucial at the middle management level when you have responsibility for a team. Perhaps it's also a matter of ego, but this is often when you see reporting being neglected. Senior management are also wary of being seen as demanding when requesting reports from those who are no longer junior employees. This is often the cause of unnecessary questions and concerns.

In today's world, we have a tool that can easily dispel such concerns. It can take just one email to report on "this is what happened." With that email, you are building a relationship of trust with your management. Anyone would be foolish not to do this. It sounds too simple to be true, but debriefing to build trust could be the most important part of every businessperson's communication strategy.

38 Analyze the situation from all angles

Every time you look at something from a new angle, you may see new problems to solve or great ideas to pursue.

Try taking a look at Rakuten Ichiba from a myriad of different angles. It is comprised of relationships between buyers and sellers but it's also a communication network, and a form of entertainment. Or you can look at it as a membership business. You can look at it as an evolution of the mail order business or as another format for use of the internet. Even if you just look at the relationship between the buyers and sellers, that prompts new questions of "What defines consumption?" and "What does it mean to sell something?"

Even a slight adjustment to the angle of your analysis can reveal a completely new perspective. What you see could be a complex problem, or it could be a game-changing idea.

Such analysis is a crucial step in advancement from the stage of mastering tasks you've been assigned to by others and reaching the stage of seeking out work for yourself. In a growing company, sooner or later you will be left behind unless you develop this analytical skill. You will only be recognized as a full member of the team when you reach the stage where you can seek out work for yourself.

Not every individual in every company thinks like this. The *salaryman,* as we call him in Japan, doesn't do this. The salaryman simply thinks his time is a paycheck. He commits units of time to collect a salary without any sense of ownership. In this sense, many executives and bureaucrats also belong to this group. It is a sad way to think and live. It can be a corrosive mindset. Sooner or later, salarymen choose to only view things from perspectives that suit them, and this is a conscious choice. Although fully aware that there are more productive ways of working, they refuse to challenge themselves. They probably think that this would only increase their workload, and they don't feel vested in taking on additional responsibilities.

It's an awful thing to say, but I find it hard to believe that any of us would choose to lead such lives. By reframing how we think about work, we can discover so much more about what we should be doing. With that attitude, we will never experience the joy of having accomplished something worthwhile. They'll reach the end of their lives without truly knowing the deep fulfillment of being energized by work.

Don't succumb to the salaryman mindset. Life is too short. Instead, develop the habit of viewing your workday within a company from multiple angles. Don't view your job from just one mundane perspective, but know it from the vantage of opportunities you can create for yourself and others. If you do, you'll see various points for improvement that you hadn't noticed before, and you'll come up with new ideas. From a salaryman's perspective, you may say this is increasing your workload, but this is an essential step in progressing beyond work as a repetitive routine, to work that you will find truly valuable, meaningful, and rewarding.

An analytic mindset can benefit you anytime and anywhere. This is true at any stage of one's career. I remember when I was a young employee at IBJ. My work in the currency department was sometimes not very challenging—there were many rote tasks to accomplish. But when I took an alternative perspective, I could see opportunities. Instead of looking at my job from my own perspective, I opted to view it from the point of view of the work group that had to process my orders. This was a group of women in a largely clerical team. Viewing my own job from their perspective, I was able to make changes in my own paperwork processing so that it made their jobs easier and more efficient. This made them happy with me and I felt a sense of accomplishment—I had made a rote experience one that could actually bring value to the company. I continue to use this process today. We are expanding our offices in Silicon Valley. I could give the instructions as to what I think the office space needs, to fit my own needs. But I am also trying to see the space from the point of view of my employees—what could we do that would improve their abilities to be more productive and happy at work?

Work isn't about solving problems given to you by others, like in an exam when you were at school. Work is about identifying problems and solving them. Solve those problems. Repeat. This is not only the essence of work, but also where you can find true joy in your work.

39 Know who and what works, even in tight spots

When a once-successful work team stumbles and results decline, it can be so easy to throw in the towel. You may start to think your team and even your company is a lost cause. But never overreact. Your dismay may be premature, and giving in to it is a self-fulfilling prophecy. No matter how bad things get, you can always find an encouraging indicator—one that might suggest a new direction in which to pivot. Let these indicators be the impetus for change and renewal.

Trust me, I know this from experience. As I've often repeated, when Rakuten Ichiba was founded, total sales in our first month amounted to ¥320,000 (about US$2,700). Of this, my own purchases amounted to ¥180,000 (US$1,500) so, in actual fact, our 13-store shopping mall had actually only generated sales of ¥140,000 (US$1,200). This wasn't just a tough spot; some thought we were finished when we'd hardly even started. But that's not how I was thinking. From my point of view, the glass was half full, not half empty. We had achieved sales of ¥140,000 in a short period of time and I saw many indicators that we could duplicate those results over and over.

I was choosing to look at the positive indicator. Most in Japan at that time believed consumers would never shop via the internet. But ¥140,000 was an indicator that physical stores were vulnerable to disruption. I opted to look in that direction.

Did we sell fourteen ¥10,000 items? Or 1,400 items at ¥100 each? What kind of customers bought from us? What did they buy, and why? You couldn't tell just by looking at the ¥140,000 sales figure. If I'd not analyzed this data, I could have just shrugged in disappointment at the total figure. But I knew there had to be reasons why people spent ¥140,000 on our platform. We needed to drill deeper to see what was actually happening.

No matter how many times you multiply zero, the answer is zero. But our results were not zero. Our results were ¥140,000. My thinking was that if we could find out why people had made those purchases, we could work to build on that ¥140,000, perhaps even a hundred times.

It was this can-do attitude amplified by everyone's hard work that made Rakuten what it is today. We didn't stop at magnifying that number a hundred times. We kept pushing forward, looking for the new indicators every day. Twenty years after that first month, our total annual gross merchandise sales in domestic e-commerce hit over 3 trillion Japanese yen (around US$30 billion).

Some companies are successful even in the worst recession. Some people and departments are successful no matter how poorly their companies are performing. Just as Hope was left behind in Pandora's Box, there's always a seed of hope somewhere. Seek it out.

It is the people and departments who are successful in the worst of times who hold the key to future success. While others may succumb to the feeling of defeat, they are the ones who are always looking for the opportunities for success.

40 Be courageous

Every startup is an adventure and a challenge. Embrace the adventure you are on. If you lose the inspiration to take on new challenges, you will also lose most of the joy in your work. And no matter how much success you achieve, eventually someone will beat you. History shows the proof of this. For startups like Rakuten in particular, if we forget this spirit, our very reason for existence in society will be lost.

Being a startup is about forging a path through the wilderness and conquering unclimbed peaks. It's about challenging the unknown and bringing new value into the world, and about that new value contributing to the happiness of the world at large. This is the very core of our work.

Creating new value isn't easy. Huge difficulties always lie in the way. But these difficulties fuel growth. Startups are successful precisely because they overcome those difficulties. There's no true success in a world where difficulties don't exist. Of course, there's no guarantee of success. We are striving to solve problems that have yet to be solved. The problems that already have answers can be left to others. A startup is about taking on the challenges that others can't, or addressing the issues that only you can. This is something I always take into account when I look at the growth potential of a startup. When I first heard from the founders of Lyft why they had started their ridesharing business, I knew that they had a compelling mission—to improve our lives by changing the way we all interact with transportation—and a promising future.

Nothing in this world is impossible. Believe in yourself, believe in those around you. Think with all your wisdom and ability, and work with all your might to make the impossible possible. Think as you forge ahead, and forge ahead in order to think. Succeed at what others have not yet succeeded at. This is the startup spirit that gives you the courage to take on challenges. No matter how much growth you achieve or how successful you are, this spirit must never be forgotten.

4

Get Your Organization Moving

You'll never achieve truly great success or deliver on big projects if you can't effectively move your organization. Learn how to develop teams and get your organization moving.

41 Numbers give clarity, so set KPIs

Key performance indicators (KPIs) are just a way of expressing goals in detail with numbers. To achieve our major objectives, we set goals for the steps along the way, and KPI is simply the term we use to refer to those concrete numerical goals.

Major objectives are crucial to influencing the direction of an organization. But to achieve those major objectives, the goals that represent steps along the way to their achievement must also be clearly laid out and visible. Unless all members of the organization understand the progress they have made against those goals, there's a possibility they will lose sight of the path. KPIs are simply the markers along that path.

In sales, for example, you can set KPIs for numbers of new contracts or new clients, expressing detailed KPIs in numbers for each of the actions that are key to achieving your major objectives.

As an organization grows, it's quite common for individual members of the team to come to feel that their role in achieving major objectives is relatively unimportant. This is when it can become almost inevitable for some members to feel that it won't make a big difference to the whole organization if they take it easy for a day. But this is the sort of thinking that, if left unchecked, will slow down the entire organization.

KPIs are the vital links between not only the major initiatives of an organization and the individual tasks of each employee but also between the major objectives that will take years to achieve and the smaller goals to be achieved today.

By setting specific numerical targets, hard numbers bolted to reality, each individual team member can track his or her own progress on a daily basis. It might be unglamorous work, but it fuels the engine of every dynamic organization.

Ultimately, the work of any company, no matter how large, is only the sum of the work done by every individual employee. If every employee in a company of 5,000 takes one step forward in one day, the organization will take 5,000 steps forward that day. Maintaining that pace over a whole year adds up to more than 1.5 million steps. To be sure you achieve those 1.5 million steps, however, every single employee must take that one step forward every day.

Some say that the success of a startup all comes down to the ideas they're able to generate. That thinking probably also means that, even if the organization is not yet developed, startups can succeed as long as their ideas are good. On the other hand, that's like saying that even successful startups with great ideas don't have great people.

That is not the kind of startup I set out to establish.

My goal wasn't to win based on ideas alone but to develop the abilities of every individual team member to a level that means we're able to disrupt and beat even the most established firms. That's another reason that I believe objective numerical goals, in the form of KPIs, are crucial. The data are clear; KPIs can drive innovation in organizations and push them to higher levels of efficiency and execution. Never take your eye off the numbers.

42 Pay close attention to resource allocation

Whether you're budgeting your time or your money, be concrete, not conceptual.

Resource allocation is all about deciding how to allocate resources to individual businesses. Paying close attention to this is vital for all companies, large or small.

Company resources will vary according to the industry, but the most important resources and what all companies have in common are human resources and capital. How should you allocate people and money? While we should all be aware of these as top priorities, surprisingly enough, many of us don't pay enough attention to the details. Allocation is often guided by vague concepts like *management know-how*—in other words, simple intuition.

Resource allocation is crucial not just for managers but for all of us. It's a question of how to best allocate and use resources with defined limits.

On an individual level, would you logically consider how to allocate your own resources, such as your time and money? You may actually need to budget both. To do this effectively, you need to take into account the total amount of resources and the needs of individual businesses. In practice, however, allocation decisions are often made on an ad hoc basis.

There was a time when I used to wake up an hour early every morning to study English before work. I don't think I'd have been able to keep it up if I'd decided to do it for an hour between getting home and going to bed. Sometimes you work late or are invited out for a drink. I was a "salaryman" and had to get up at a certain time every day anyway. Getting up an hour earlier wasn't as hard as you'd imagine, as you'll learn once you try it. It's actually easy to wake up two or even three hours earlier than you need to. Among high-performance workers in the United States and Europe, it's not unusual to show up for work at four or five in the morning. At such an early hour, no one calls, there are no meetings, and no one bothers you for anything. You can be incredibly efficient at this time of the day. If you can get your day's deskwork done before everyone else even turns up, you can use the rest of your day much more effectively. In central Tokyo, there's also the added bonus of missing the morning rush hour. It may be a small thing, but it's these things that can revitalize your everyday life and open up great new possibilities.

The same recommendation applies when you look at resource allocation for organizations. Always questioning common sense and being consistently rational are indispensable. For example, don't assign lots of top people to a particular department just because it's an important part of the company. Sometimes assigning a smaller number of enthusiastic young people with less experience to a task can yield better results. This can happen because abilities are not static, and, depending on the environment and circumstances, you can sometimes see unrealized talent bloom. The right mix of veterans and newcomers can be a catalyst for major change. Human resources should always be on the lookout for this human chemistry. It's a process a computer can't duplicate.

I fully understand that individual observations in team creation become difficult to put into practice as company scale grows. It's when organizations become large that their ability to resolve personnel issues and high performance teams within the organization becomes even more crucial to future growth.

Resource allocation can never become a routine or rote process. It must always be viewed as dynamic and rooted in human insight, yet grounded by rationality.

43 Lead by teaching

A leader is a commander and strategist, but also a teacher. This is true for every leader, no matter how small the group.

Particularly when you're young, you tend to think of leaders only as commanders. But a true leader does more than just command a team. Leaders are strategists and must be aware of the greater context of their team's role: They must always plan out the overarching strategy, not just work out tactically on the immediate issues at hand—just as skiers on the slopes must look both at what lies ahead and the terrain beneath them. If you lose sight of where you're going and why, you can't lead your team in the right direction. What's more, if you don't think strategically, you won't be able to formulate an appropriate response when an unexpected situation arises, when mistakes are inevitably made and trouble presents itself.

We all know that cutting our losses is the best way to cope with failure. But not all failures are the same. If there were only one type of loss, it would probably not be too difficult to respond to it. However, complex businesses generate various kinds of losses: impacting earnings, customer trust, and team spirit, among other things. So the question is—which losses should you strive to minimize right now? You must think strategically to make the correct decision. That's why it's often said that the best commanders are those who excel at fighting from a losing position, like the Duke of Wellington in the early 1800s.

Another leadership mandate we shouldn't forget is that great leaders must also be teachers. Natural leaders are confident in their actions and judgment. What takes a leader from good to great is the ability to pass on these skills.

It's the same in sport: Great athletes don't necessarily make great coaches. It's difficult to teach others things that you can do intuitively. And it's extremely hard if there's a difference in natural talent between you and the individual you're teaching.

When asked about how to be a good batter in baseball, the Japanese baseball icon Shigeo Nagashima once said, "You just hit the ball when it comes toward you." This is something that only a genius would say. These 10 words express the very essence of batting, but this is difficult for an ordinary ballplayer or fan to understand. The natural talent of a genius must be broken down into parts so that an average person can understand it.

Your intuition as a leader can't be widely understood until you can articulate it in a teachable way. Teaching can come in actions or words (which is one of my reasons for writing this book).

You can't create a good company simply by bringing lots of talented people together. Because when one leaves, your company will suffer in proportion. You need to construct a framework to transfer abilities. This isn't simply a question of passing on knowledge. I don't think a company can claim to be educating its employees until the ability of all employees as a whole are enhanced. A company won't last long without a system that continually educates its employees.

What drives your successes? Conduct a thorough analysis, and once you understand that, be a teacher and communicate this to your team members. Develop your team and achieve your goals. Then aim higher.

The ability to set a positive cycle in motion like this is the hallmark of a true leader. It all starts with a commitment to educate others.

44 Leverage the organization to move faster

There are many complaints out there about organizations. People say they become rigid, that they stop working. Criticism of bureaucracy is similar. But it's pathetic when colleagues within organizations resort to these complaints. I want to remind them that getting their organization moving is their own job.

Organizations exist to enable us to achieve things we can't accomplish alone. Members of organizations should view their organizations as their foundational tools. I want to say to them, you should be able to use that tool! Drivers keep their cars maintained and filled with gasoline. Chefs sharpen their knives daily to ensure precision. You'll never hear professional chefs say they can't cook because their knives are dull. Professionals know it's their job to be prepared. An organization is a tool a million times more complicated than a knife or a car, so it's obvious that if we don't continue to innovate and make an effort to get an organization moving, it will stop functioning effectively.

We must constantly be innovating and making an effort to drive our organizations forward. Sometimes drastic steps are needed to revive a stagnant organization. If an organization is too idle or inefficient, the first step is to eliminate waste to reclaim speed. It's my observation that most organizations could move 10 times faster simply by identifying and cutting waste.

Make this your personal aim. Reduce the time spent in meetings, or whatever, by 90 percent. Cut a two-hour meeting to 12 minutes. You'll probably say that this is impossible, but really make the effort to achieve it. You may surprise yourself.

Everyone's attitude will change when they realize their organization is working 10 times faster. And they'll start to feel motivated, because, if you're going to run, running faster is even more fun. Work is boring if you're dawdling. And once you realize how fast you can run, you will start to feel an intense craving to run even more. It's when people feel this urge that the whole organization will move.

Some may think wrapping up a two-hour meeting in 12 minutes is impossible. But I did it at Rakuten. The actual decision-making part of a meeting only takes five minutes or less. The remaining time is taken up by explanations. In such cases, the explanations could be written down. I made those who wanted to speak at meetings submit what they wanted to say in writing a day before the meeting—something they would have had to present anyway. This added to their workload (although only slightly), as they had to submit a clean copy in advance. Those attending meetings read all the submissions before the meeting starts. They can easily do this when they have a spare moment. So at the actual meeting we have five minutes to clear up any questions, five minutes to make decisions, and two minutes to spare.

Some colleagues of mine had trouble with this in the beginning, but the system is now working very smoothly. Writing something down rather than saying it clarifies the weaknesses and vague points in any argument. The system has also made everyone skilled at clearly summarizing the key points. A byproduct of the system is that the content of meetings is far more significant.

An organization will move 10 times faster if you really want it to. And the faster it moves, the more effective it will be.

45 Harness the power of competition

Darwin's theory of evolution posits natural selection as a law of the natural world, but introducing this law into your enterprise will also make it evolve. In other words, leverage the power of constructive competition within your organization. Many companies already do this, although whether they are doing it correctly is open to debate. After all, two colleagues trying to pull each other down is one form of competition. One may lose, the other may win, but in the end, the company is no better off. So I believe it's important to create not just a competitive environment but also an environment in which competition is net positive for company growth.

You must therefore create an environment in which harnessing the power of competition draws out those abilities and drives motivation. At Rakuten's headquarters, for the use of all employees, I've created a library as a self-study space, with educational programs, and a fitness gym. Exercise is a good way of relieving stress, but it's also a way to grow. In order to be effective at work, you need more than just your brain working.

Of course, everyone is free to choose to use, or not to use, the facilities. Sadly, many employees are too busy to use them, but I think this also shows that the competitive principle is working naturally at Rakuten—no matter how busy things are, there's always someone who manages to find the time to lift weights in the gym or read an educational book in the library. Of course, they don't have to do these things at work. What's important for us as a company is that we express to every employee that we are keen to see them grow. The facilities are a physical expression of this mindset.

There's a stark difference between someone who's always strived to grow and someone who hasn't. If the environment is conducive to growth, employees will realize that improving their abilities is an effective way of boosting their results. Those who don't will be left behind in the process of natural selection. Once that kind of environment exists, it's important to build a framework for competition.

The Rakuten corporate culture is intensely competitive. We reward those who achieve outstanding results, recognizing their performance, and conversely we give negative evaluations to those who don't perform. A system of demerit, however, is not part of our culture. Taking on a challenge and failing is not a sign of weakness and we don't play the blame game when that happens.

Doing nothing, on the other hand, is not something that will garner praise. Always doing the same thing is simply not good enough. Whatever your position in the company, every individual should be setting and testing hypotheses in order to achieve even better results. You will get marked down for not continuing to make this effort.

Getting marked down doesn't just mean a pay cut. There have been times when executives have been demoted to the status of regular employees. However, it's possible to make a comeback at any time. Rack up enough positive evaluations in your new position and there is no limit to how far you can advance.

This is not an easy environment to work in for those used to handling only the tasks they are served. In my company, employees are expected to seek out and solve new problems.

Those who realize that being in this kind of environment will improve their own abilities are the ones who excel and thrive. Professional growth and promotion become a major motivation driving their work. Indeed, there's no greater joy in life than knowing you have improved.

46 Share the sense of accomplishment

A "sense of accomplishment" is not an empty expression but a feeling much more profound than the one you experience in response to a financial reward. It's even deeper when we achieve something together with our colleagues.

I'm not discounting the importance of financial rewards. It's the source of the energy that drives and builds companies. If a company can't make a profit, it will eventually wither away. I started Rakuten because I wanted to achieve something big, but I certainly needed money to do it. Obviously, the pursuit of profit is at the core of why companies exist.

It's the same for every individual employee. We work to earn an income. However, a purely financial reward is not enough to bring out our true strengths. This may be a little idealistic, but I believe human beings are essentially creatures who feel even greater joy when we accomplish something as a team. I don't know how many tens of thousands of years it's been since our ancestors came out of the jungles and began to hunt in tribes, but that's how we've been living ever since. We've spent our lives in tribes, in groups, in teams. There's no doubt that we've always experienced that special joy of achieving things as a group. If you consider the context of humankind's staggeringly long history, currency as a means of exchange for value is something that only came into existence very recently. So it's understandable that the joy of monetary gain doesn't connect with our primal roots.

Sharing a sense of collaborative accomplishment is a fundamental driver of corporate growth. The joy of achieving something together with those close to you fosters development of new talent and enables companies to reach stretch goals. That's why there should always be a sense of sharing the joy of accomplishment in the workplace. And it's beyond doubt that the greater the achievement, the greater the joy.

One year, I challenged 170 new Rakuten employees fresh out of college to reach a quota for signing up new customers for Rakuten credit cards. I gave them one month to sign up 10 new customers each. I assumed that even these young people could achieve this goal.

My corporate training challenge didn't turn out as I anticipated. None of them achieved the goal. I was horrified. They weren't able to do something that should have been possible to do with a small effort because they didn't put in that effort. I decided to test them. I gave them one more week, but also said that in return they had to secure 30 contracts each.

If they hadn't been able to win 10 contracts in a month, why would I challenge them to reach a seemingly ridiculous goal—three times the metric they'd just failed to achieve? But I had my reason. I knew that we can achieve just about anything if we really put our minds to it. Our true strengths come to the fore when we're racing toward that impossible goal.

The 170 new employees returned at the end of the week with 10,000 contracts, or 58.8 per person. I was speechless.

But I was also secretly enjoying imagining the looks on their faces when they realized their achievement. Did they hug and slap each other on the back, the way my generation did? They learned that they can achieve any goal, no matter how difficult, if they put their heads together as a team.

Humanity is where it is today because we have worked toward major goals, encouraging those we work with, being encouraged, and opening up new paths together. In this way, we've made the impossible possible and pushed past our boundaries. There is no greater joy to be experienced at work than this. When I first announced that our company would make English our language of business, I knew it would be a huge challenge to achieve that goal. It was often difficult, it took longer than expected, and many people along the way said I was crazy. But when employees in our company did start achieving successful English test scores, when meetings could be run in English as a matter of course, and when other major companies began to look at our experience as a model for their own English language programs, I felt that sense of achievement—the one that only comes when you've pushed yourself farther than anyone thought you could go.

47 Find the bottlenecks

No division in any company is ever really working at 100 percent efficiency. They all have their own issues and weaknesses. It's important to eliminate weaknesses, but there's something even more important that you must do first. Among all the deficiencies you see, you must find out which of them reduce efficiency of the company. Find the bottlenecks. If you don't address the bottlenecks, other attempts at improving the company may be ineffectual or even meaningless.

Put the other way around, resolving bottlenecks boosts overall efficiency. A relatively small effort has a major impact. It should be your first step.

Constantly examine your overall operation and develop an eye for bottlenecks in workflow. This is useful personally, not just for organizations. For example, thinking about where the bottlenecks are in your own work can be a springboard to drive higher performance.

Sometimes, right when you think everything in your company is going well, you'll encounter a surprise bottleneck. In 2007, Rakuten moved its headquarters to new premises. A large proportion of headquarter functions were consolidated in Rakuten Tower, a building in Shinagawa, Tokyo. Some 5,000 employees worked in the 23-story building. The building had

10 elevators working around the clock. But at peak hours, the elevators presented a transportation bottleneck. The elevator hall was always crowded during the morning rush and around the regular Tuesday morning company-wide meeting. It could take up to 30 minutes to get all 5,000 people back to their seats after the meeting. Everyone started the day feeling irritated in the crowded elevator hall, waiting to ride the elevator. While I appreciated that everyone was committed to making efforts to improve their work efficiency, as we were always talking about it, it also looked like everyone had given up on the elevator problem and had resigned themselves to waiting patiently. I bristled with my own impatience, watching everyone shuffling around waiting for the elevator. The 30 minutes it took to get everyone through the elevators was a complete waste of time. Thirty minutes per person meant we were losing 2,500 working hours right there. If we couldn't solve such a simple problem as the elevators, how could we aim to be number one in the world?

We attacked the problem by the numbers. The congested elevators stopped on every floor, and when we did the calculations, we realized it took 20 seconds to let off passengers on each floor. For one elevator to go up to the top floor and back, stopping on every floor took as much as an extra 440 seconds.

So I decided the elevator in a building of 23 stories would only make 10 stops: on 1, 2, 3, 5, 7, 10, 13, 14, 17, and 21. Those who worked on a floor at which the elevator didn't stop were to get off at a nearby floor and use the stairs. (Of course, the stop buttons were still accessible for people with disabilities.)

This system reduced the time it took to transport everyone back to their desks to less than five minutes. This small gain boosted workforce productivity by 5 percent. Also, we didn't just reduce the amount of time lost. Without a doubt, we also eliminated the stress and frustration of our elevator rush hour.

Don't ignore bottlenecks, no matter how trivial they may seem. Resolving them can lead to improvements that ripple throughout the organization.

48 Create your own turning point

The nodes in a bamboo stalk are the secret to its powerful growth. There are times when companies also need to create such nodes, or turning points. There are times when even though you're working as hard as ever, growth slows and indicators seem to stop rising altogether. This is the nature of growth. Growth doesn't happen in a straight line but actually ratchets upward, like steps. As there will be plateaus, you should make good use of those times when growth flattens out. Slow growth periods can be used for reflection and planning next steps.

Say you teach a group of children how to add and subtract, then get them to practice what they've learned. At first, the more they practice, the more skilled they become. But at some point they stop improving no matter how much they practice. That's when it's time to move up a step and teach them how to multiply and divide.

In education, you know what to teach at what stage. But it is difficult when it comes to corporate growth, because every company is entirely different from every other company. It's not as simple a remedy as moving on from addition to multiplication. It's more common for companies to tread water during plateau periods while they search for a breakthrough. In many cases, they can even start going backward when they can't find a way of getting past the plateau. Even if you want to try something new, you have little access to capital and human resources and few options because your rate of growth has slowed.

When I say create the turning point, I mean create an artificial plateau when you're one or even two steps short of the natural plateau—in other words, while you're still growing. Stop for a second, rethink the state and direction of your company, and prepare for the next stage. For example, cut costs or personnel before it becomes absolutely necessary. Or switch to completely new ways of doing things.

Companies usually only do this when earnings have peaked and have started to deteriorate. But I recommend doing it while they're still growing. You need courage to do this when things are going well. You might face a torrent of competitive opposition. However, if you plan your strategy when you're growing, when you have ample financial and human resources, your new iterations and ideas will progress far more efficiently. As you grow, you can make internal changes and move smoothly on to the next growth stage.

Aim for further substantial growth by creating these reflective turning points, rather than waiting for the crisis of the real plateau.

49 Meet and revive in the morning

Every department at Rakuten has a daily morning meeting. Team members share information to understand current conditions within the department. At the beginning of the day, we clarify the theme and objectives of the day's work. Departments that do this well are without exception tremendously successful.

Generally speaking, failures in business usually occur when people get sloppy. They stop planning and using themes and objectives and as a result, their work lacks clarity. To regain clarity, think: "What should I do today?" and "What should I do tomorrow?" Organize your work into a sequence of events.

However, if you don't prioritize and establish a clear plan of action, you are setting yourself up for failure. Essentially, you are wandering without a compass. You work for 8 hours, from 9 to 5. If you work without some sense of direction, you can waste the whole day without doing anything meaningful. Do it every day and you may go years without accomplishing anything.

Morning meetings create milestones that give clarity to your everyday work. Whether we like to admit it or not, all of us can lapse into laziness. If there's an opportunity, we take it easy. I know this because I'm like that, too. To ensure such opportunities don't arise, it's important to stimulate your motivation with a daily agenda at the start of each day.

If you have clear goals for action, not only will you be building up that motivation, you will have to focus on your work, whether you like it or not. If you focus, you'll accomplish more than you even thought possible. What's more, as you continue to experience this, you'll find work will become enjoyable.

You might find setting specific goals at the start of every day troublesome to begin with. But if you persevere, you'll probably realize it makes your work even more rewarding and meaningful. I recommend it to anyone and everyone. If you're not in a position to call morning meetings, you can "meet" with yourself and take a few minutes to establish your priorities and goals for the day. At the start of the day, clearly organize your goals for that day, and take steps to achieve those goals. You'll be astounded at what this disciplined approach will produce over weeks, months, even a full career.

50 Think like a manager

In Japan, there is an expression that refers to "the salaryman mindset." As described in Chapter 3, it is used to describe people who think of themselves as nothing more than workers for hire who only need to do what they're paid for. The salaryman never volunteers for an assignment or pushes himself to excel beyond stated expectations. He never thinks about his role in the company and how he could do better. He never does more or less than absolutely necessary. I have a hard time believing anyone can be happy with a salaryman mindset. It's my belief that a manager mindset—no matter what your actual title may be—is far more fulfilling.

Having a manager's mindset means ridding yourself of this salaryman spirit. In other words, it means feeling that the company you work for is your company. You see things differently when you do business with a manager's mindset. You can see the big picture of the business as a whole and you understand your role in the larger success of the firm.

Cultivating this mindset isn't a question of ability. It's a question of perspective. The man who stands on the roof of a building can see farther than the man on the ground. It's not because he has naturally better eyesight; it's because he sought out the vantage point that allowed him the broader view.

Why does a manager mindset give you a wider perspective? To put it simply, it's because when you look at your business as a manager you will see the overall balance between income and expenditure. As a result, you will understand how each specific individual job connects to the overall sales and profits of the company. Connecting the dots this way is empowering. Great companies are able to instill this mindset in virtually every employee. This is what management is all about. If you think like a manager, you will always come back to this perspective. It will give you the benefit of a big-picture perspective.

For some, the issue is all about money. In Japan, some avoid a direct focus on money, thinking it's somehow not virtuous. People who fuss about money can end up being disliked.

But any CEO must be fussy about money and a manager mindset requires it, too. Business is, at its core, all about money. In the war that is business, money can be compared to weapons and ammunition. It's impossible to consider overall strategy without money taking center stage. Managers think of this first.

Most employees don't think about it at all. As a result, their perspective on the company narrows. When this happens, they can't see what lies ahead.

Always think like a manager to achieve a bird's-eye perspective. This will give your daily work clarity and make it much more interesting and fulfilling. When all employees have this mindset, a company will soar.

51 Create and share a template for success

There are winning patterns to be found everywhere. Success in one field allows you to develop a template for success that can be applied in other fields, based on a thorough understanding of the reasons behind the success.

Rakuten Ichiba was our first success at Rakuten. We tried various things to achieve success. We then identified which of those things were effective. These initiatives included providing different services to merchants opening stores, launching a loyalty points program, sometimes cutting costs to achieve these initiatives, and rolling out marketing tactics. Many of those things were effective. Combined together, we codified them and called it our template for success. This is a template we carry forward as we enter into new businesses.

The effort required to make a business successful is sobering. Some studies say 80 percent of all new businesses fail. If you succeed, you will be among the minority whose efforts are rewarded. But, on its own, this initial success of any new venture means nothing. If you establish a template for success by trying various things and figuring out what works and what doesn't, however, you can apply that template to other projects.

Most well-established companies do this. However, many start-ups never reach that point. Perhaps because they're sure their initial success depends on an original idea, one that would be hard to replicate. But, if we leave aside for a moment the surprise hit products and the cyclical boom periods, there will always be a logical reason why success has come to a business. That logical reason is what you want to capture in a template.

If you can organize your pattern for success into a template, it becomes a valuable company asset. You will need to break down your experience and investigate deeply—often, the pattern may not be readily visible on the surface. Why did that go well? Why were we successful? What are the unique factors, what are the universal factors? You must dig deep and analyze the reasons, and find a pattern that can be applied to in other areas.

If you can do this, you'll find the results can also be applied at an individual level. Whenever something goes well, figure out why and draw up a pattern which you can apply in other cases. Your method of studying English (in my case, making regular time to practice) could even improve your golf game. And it did. Applying the template I drew from my English worked in golf. So create templates. It's a method with wide applications.

52 Earn trust within your company

Soccer players must earn their teammates' trust in order to play well themselves. Players who aren't trusted by their teammates never receive a pass. They can't be counted upon to convert to a goal. They are known to break the chain of connection. No matter how good they are, they won't be able to utilize their talent if they never get a chance to kick the ball.

This lesson from the soccer field applies in business. I have heard colleagues say, "No matter what I say, no one listens." They claim their work doesn't go well because no one listens to them. In other words, it's not their own fault, but the fault of everyone else who apparently refuses to listen.

If you're engaging in this kind of thinking, you're likely misguided. That coworkers and subordinates aren't listening to you is a problem, to be sure. But don't fault the audience; fault the messenger.

If you remove yourself from the situation and think about it from a third-person perspective, it's immediately obvious. Think of someone you know who can't get others to listen to them. There must be a reason why people are not listening. Now think of someone who people do listen carefully to—what kind of person are they?

Working in a company is a team effort. Just like in soccer, you can't do a good job if your team members don't trust you. So, earning the trust of close colleagues is also an important part of your job.

If you work in a company, strive to be that person about whom colleagues say, "Leave it up to them. It'll be fine, and if they can't do it, no one can."

The ability to earn the trust of your colleagues is a key work competency.

53 Establish symbolic rituals

No one would argue that determination is not a winning trait. I agree, but at the same time, I don't generally put my faith in the determination of others. Human beings often lack the strength and discipline to maintain a state of determination. Someone can be intensely fired up about an issue one day and forget it the next. That's just how we are.

It's important to understand these human tendencies and to create structures that help us confront them. None of us wants to forget the passions or burning ambitions that inspire us now. But we know, based on human behavior, that even those intense passions will eventually cool if left untended.

Symbolic rituals can guard against that. They may seem at first to be somewhat meaningless actions. But in fact, they provide the structure and support to keep passion alive.

We have many symbolic rituals at Rakuten. For example, every Monday, we have a companywide morning meeting called Asakai, after which employees clean their desks. We've been doing this since we started Rakuten Ichiba with just a handful of employees.

It's one ritual that serves to remind everyone that we are a team working to realize everyone's dreams. Six employees have grown to more than 14,000, but by gathering and participating in the ritual, we are able to connect and feel the presence of our co-workers.

This isn't just about establishing traditions. Symbolic rituals, such as everyone cleaning desks together and attending regular morning meetings, foster a sense of unity among staff. Moreover, regularly confirming one's own corporate culture via such customs establishes a certain pace, like a musical rhythm, in the bodies known as organizations. Call them rituals for the corporate soul.

Concepts like milestones and codes of conduct are said to be old hat. But I don't think human beings are strong enough to do away with these entirely. Our corporate culture has impact on our ability to succeed. No matter how passionate you are about your ambitions or ideals, you'll forget them eventually if you don't keep them close to your heart.

That's why our Monday mornings will always be about Asakai and cleaning our desks afterward. That way we won't forget our ideals and aspirations, and everyone will be united.

I'd wager no one is born with strong self-discipline. So it's all the more to your credit when you overcome those weaknesses to achieve something. Organizations are the same. No matter how lofty a person's ideals, how dedicated to their company they claim to be, those things alone are meaningless. It's much more important to establish everyday rituals that help to unite everyone's hearts and minds in a common rhythm.

54 Successful organizations combine pressure and excitement

Work without a sense of excitement is as bland as food without spice. The more excitement you feel at work, the more likely you are to become engrossed in it.

The issue is how to generate that sense of excitement in the workplace. The answer is common goals. As human beings, we draw joy from the experience of achieving something. To feel that joy of achievement, you must first set that goal.

The reason that organizations without goals are unsuccessful is that they lack the constructs to feed off each other's energy. It is only when you share common goals that a random group of people will come together to form a coherent organization. The feeling that we are all working together to achieve a higher objective is what connects and inspires us. That's the energy that gives a workplace its own unique buzz.

Ideally, everyone feels like they're running together as fast as they can to reach a goal that almost seems unattainable. Fear dissipates. Action takes over. A sense of excitement and energy in the workplace takes over.

That said, excitement alone won't bring success. The workplace needs a second factor to harness that excitement and funnel it in the right direction. And that additional factor is pressure. Often, pressure is seen as a negative aspect of work life. But in combination with excitement, the right amount of pressure is good. It sharpens the mind and makes you aware of the details, which are important at work. The pressure is what keeps people on their toes.

You can't do really excellent work unless you're concerned about every single aspect of it, however small. That's why every member of an organization must work continually to sharpen their senses, and why organizations also need to create an environment with the right amount of pressure. This can feel like stress and managers must be alert for this and strive for the right balance. The right amount of pressure can also motivate you to achieve. It is part of a leader's responsibility to apply that pressure to the whole organization. Sometimes I will deliberately use tough language to jolt the team into action. A team without a sense of urgency drives me crazy because I know it is missing the key ingredient to success. You must approach your work, convinced that the very survival of the company is dependent on you.

Excitement and pressure: They're like the two wheels on a bike. Only when both wheels are turning will your company come to life.

55 Know that there are two types of speed: velocity and agility

To me, there are two kinds of speed: velocity and agility. Velocity is about sheer speed, whereas agility is about your ability to respond at explosive speed.

In work terms, we can increase *velocity* with measures for improving the efficiency of daily tasks, like shortening meetings, cutting the number of copies we make, or reducing the number of people working on a project.

In fact, I think it would be safe to say that we waste 70 percent of each day. This is waste that we must reduce. And not just once. Waste is like household garbage: Even if you throw it out in the morning, it builds up again by evening. So you have to keep on throwing it out. Waste is a monster that reduces efficiency in the workplace. Waste slows decision making. Do away with waste and decision making will accelerate. Even that one action will accelerate the speed of your work.

Agility, the other type of speed, might also be called *explosive speed*. Athletes talk about this all the time. This is the burst of speed that leads to a goal or a game-changing event. This is the speed that launches you into action once you've made the decision to move. Once you've decided to do something, move quickly. When I talk about the importance of being quick on your feet, I'm also talking about agility.

Agility is particularly crucial when you change direction in your work. You naturally lose speed when you change direction. Uncertainty and fear will slow you down even further, but these things are not external, they are rooted in your mind. And you won't be able to regain speed until you focus on reality. So you should move as quickly you can to do so. The best course of action is to close your mind to your fear and get moving. This will cause you to think—you will think as you move. When I start something, first I get up and start running straight ahead. There's no point fussing around. I just get running. Then everyone will come chasing after me. I know that by the time the team catches up with me, everyone will be working at top speed. It's how quickly everyone gets up to top speed that determines the agility of the organization: That explosive speed is a vital skill.

Attempts to change direction often fail because they slow companies down. Loss of speed can be lethal to an organization. Loss of speed has caused many failures and disasters. We all naturally slow down when we change direction. Success depends on how quickly we can recover from that and reach top speed again. Even if the organization fails at something, if it's moving quickly, the potential for recovery is much greater.

Velocity and agility: two kinds of speed. An outstanding organization must have both.

56 Divide into small groups to improve transparency

Making shelves larger makes it harder to see what's stored on them.

Companies are the same. If one section grows very large, it becomes hard to see what's going on inside it. What's even more of an issue is that it becomes difficult to see where responsibility lies, and each individual employee's sense of accountability suffers as a result.

In nature, animals that are preyed upon are the ones that form large groups. The larger the group, the less likely it is that an animal will fall victim to the hunter. This is knowledge essential for survival. However, when human beings band into large groups, the only thing I see happening is that our sense of urgency fades and accountability suffers. When predators form groups, the groups are not usually very large. Each animal has its own responsibilities and there is no redundancy. Members of the group that aren't fulfilling a useful role in the hunt are a hindrance.

It's obvious which is better in the context of forming work teams: Work teams should be as small as possible. The number of Rakuten employees has increased by more than 2,000 times over 20 years but, as we've grown, we've divided our sections into smaller units.

At Rakuten Ichiba, merchant relations is divided into sections responsible for the different stages in the flow from recruiting to onboarding to day-to-day consulting. It's also divided by genre into groups such as fashion, sports, and food and drinks. The sports group is further divided into categories such as golf, tennis, and skiing. We also took this approach in the regions as the employee headcount increased, subdividing the Kansai region into Osaka, Kobe, and Kyoto.

By doing this, we've made sure that units always have only the minimum number of staff needed to do the work at hand. That's why we can clearly identify the root cause of a problem when it arises. Because responsibilities are clearly defined, decisions can be made quickly about what should be changed and how.

It goes without saying that the reverse is also true: It is very clear which unit is achieving results. This increases the feeling of accomplishment, which leads to a competitive mindset, in a good sense. It also makes it easy for other units to learn from examples of success.

Making units small increases organizational transparency. Things that you can't see in a large organization become visible. In another sense, it makes it possible to see them from an objective perspective.

Divide teams into the smallest groups possible and make clear who's responsible for what.

5

Win Every Battle

Businesspeople must produce results. To do so, they must understand the core essentials of their work. This chapter is about how to fight a hundred battles, and win every one.

57 Analyze and execute with an eye on the future
Like long grass in which a snake might be hiding, the future will always hold uncertainty. In the real world, little goes as planned.

Are there any snakes lurking in the grass you're walking through right now? If there are, what kind are they? You can't know without actually taking that walk through the grass. And if you don't make any preparations because you don't know what lies ahead, you'll just end up getting bitten. What will you do if a snake appears on the path before you? It's important to be prepared for incidents like this that are difficult to predict. You need to draw up a number of hypothetical scenarios for the way forward, and be able to respond if what you expected fails to materialize. Consider the story of US Airways Flight 1549, which struck a flock of birds minutes after takeoff from a New York airport and was forced to make a miraculous "ditch" landing in the Hudson River. Many credited the skill of the pilot, Chesley B. "Sully" Sullenberger. Captain Sullenberger himself credited his training, which included many years of practicing hypothetical ditch scenarios.

When you consider all the hypothetical scenarios and prepare for them, you plot a path to success. For example, when Rakuten Ichiba first started, merchants paid a fixed fee of ¥50,000 a month, or about US$400, the first six months of which was an upfront payment. At the time, the average monthly fee for selling via internet shopping malls was several hundred thousand yen. We went for the unusually low fee of ¥50,000 because I predicted an explosion in the number of online stores with the spread of the internet. At only ¥50,000 a month, having just 10 or 20 stores signed up wouldn't be profitable. But if the number increased to 200, 300, or more, for example, the model would become sustainable. I forecast that this would happen within two years.

This was scenario number one, so to speak. By setting the monthly fee at the low level of ¥50,000, if the future turned out as I predicted, I knew we would have merchants flocking to Rakuten Ichiba.

However, there was no guarantee that things would actually work out in line with my expectations. Even if the internet did take off as I expected, it could end up taking 10 years to get to the level my forecasts depended on.

So I drew up scenario number two. This model took into account the possibility that the internet would spread more slowly than I'd predicted. This was why we set up the system so that merchants were required to pay six months' fees in advance. This would mean cash revenues of ¥300,000 (US$2,400) when we secured a new merchant contract. This cash flow was very important, especially for a small business. With this model, even if the number of merchants grew more slowly than we expected due to slow growth in use of the internet, we could still stay in business.

In some ways, business resembles gambling. If you compare this principle of mine about developing multiple scenarios to roulette, it's like placing chips on multiple numbers. The difference between business and gambling, however, is that even if you place multiple bets, in gambling you still won't be guaranteed a win.

In business, while there's no absolute guarantee of success, you can boost your chances to nearly 100 percent. In every game of roulette, there comes a point when you can no longer place bets. In business, in the most extreme scenario, you can still place a bet even when the ball has stopped rolling and you can see where the winning chips are. You may have only placed one chip on number one, but the moment you realize that's the winning number, you can place a hundred chips on it. Of course, you can't do this if you haven't already thought to prepare the extra hundred chips.

That's why you must look into the future, draw up multiple scenarios, and make the necessary preparations to ensure you can ride any one of the waves of the opportunity that will come your way.

58 Hypothesize, then create *shikumi*

To create a process for success, draw up a hypothesis, then create a system, or as we like to say create *shikumi*.

Frankly, I think the roots of just about any type of business growth can be traced back to this approach. Actually, this goes beyond just business. To achieve any kind of growth, all you have to do is keep on repeating these two steps. And drawing up hypotheses is not the hard part; you know what steps are required to grow. For example, if you want to master Chinese, you know that you need to study the language. The difficult part is keeping at it. That's where creating *shikumi* comes into it.

Creating *shikumi* is the process of making a validated hypothesis a part of your everyday life. For example, to master Chinese, you might decide to wake up 10 minutes earlier every day to study. This is a *shikumi*. The gist of this is to make studying Chinese for 10 minutes a day part of your regular schedule. Even with this level of commitment, you should find that in a year you'll have achieved substantial results.

Recently, in order to strengthen my lower body, I've been walking up the 10 flights of stairs from one of our company meeting rooms to my office. There are 220 steps. We have two meetings in that room a week, so that makes 440 steps I climb each week. As a year has 50 work weeks, I'll climb 22,000 steps a year. I also use a pedometer to make sure I do it. To be completely accurate, I use a mobile phone with a pedometer function, allowing me to easily check my progress on exactly how many steps I've taken on any given day.

You might think there is nothing special about a pedometer, but this system has yielded outstanding results for me. I've only been doing it for a few months but I've already built up the muscle in my legs. If you implement *shikumi*, even if it's something small, and make it part of your everyday life, you are bound to see good results.

The important thing is to commit to a formal system. I don't think I'd have followed through if I'd just said I'd try to use the stairs after meetings where possible. I clearly defined this system by committing to myself that I would always use the stairs after those meetings. And I took measures to make sure I could closely track the results and keep to the system—in my case, by using a pedometer.

Similarly, every hour around the clock, I get an update on Rakuten Ichiba sales directly to my mobile phone. This is one way I've validated my hypothesis about the importance of managing the business in hourly units.

Understanding how your hypothesis plays out in real life is key to successful *shikumi*.

59 Get things done

There are only two types of people in this world: those who seek ways of achieving things, and those who make excuses for not being able to do things. So many people are the second type, but it's the first that propels society forward.

There is inevitably pain and struggle involved in achieving something. One percent of the world's population takes that on in order to accomplish things at any length, while the remaining 99 percent ride on their coattails, taking the easy road for a quiet life. These are also the people who like to put obstacles in the way of trying something new. They are also the masters of finding reasons for why things won't work out. Whatever it is, they can come up with 10 or 20 reasons why something can't be done. Nothing good comes from wasting time with these people. It's ridiculous to spend the only life you have making excuses for why you can't do things.

Should you look for excuses as to why you didn't achieve your target, or pour all your energies into seeking ways to achieve it next time? The difference between these two mindsets is the difference between heaven and earth.

A goal you are certain of achieving isn't a real goal. A goal should be set high enough that your current self can't achieve it. It is only this kind of goal that will make you stretch yourself and grow. Obviously, you won't know whether you can achieve the goal—but you must believe that you can. Go after that goal with the conviction that you will achieve it, regardless of what obstacle comes in your path, by thinking through every possible way to get there. This is the only path to personal growth and to success in business.

I don't mean to sell you a pipe dream, to say that you can make any dream come true if you just believe in it. That's not what I mean. What I'm saying here is that there's no problem that can't be solved if you put your mind to it. I know this from experience.

There's a saying that "God never gives you more than you can handle." No matter what obstacle you come up against, the fact that it has appeared before you means that you have the potential to overcome it.

More important than anything is that, however difficult the goal, you must believe you are capable of achieving it and do everything in your power to make it happen.

Utilizing wisdom and innovation, you can make the impossible possible. Nothing is more interesting than this, and it's the reason I'm so fascinated with business, to the extent that I suspect I might be a business nerd. But, the fact is, the more you do business, the more difficult the problems you face, and the more joy you get from solving them. The greater the goal, the more inspired I am. Every day I think of how exhilarating it is to lead the Rakuten Group, climbing tall mountains and the feeling of standing on the peak.

Do you see things this way? Or do you see difficult situations as something to be avoided? These are the only two attitudes to life.

60 Examine the facts from every angle

All facts must be examined from multiple perspectives. We all intuitively know this is true, but too few of us actually do it.

There is nothing more fundamentally useful to solving problems than this. I'd go so far as to say that most of the world's problems could actually be solved just by viewing them from a different perspective. Changing your perspective means looking at things from a different vantage point.

For example, think about this book you're reading. How did this book come to arrive in your hands? For this book to make its way from my pen to your hands, it went through many different processes and the hands of many intermediaries: an editor, a publisher, printer, distributor, and a bookstore or a library. Various people were responsible for different tasks at each of these stages. These people were the links in the chain to bringing this book to you. All of these people made this book possible.

What's important is that what matters about this book is different for each of these people. In some cases, the difference is slight, in other cases, substantial. And, in still other instances, there is a common goal.

For a reader, the most important thing is most likely to be the content. What's written in the book is important as it will be something from the content that will catch the interest of a potential reader and prompt them to buy or borrow a book. For someone at the shipping company, however, this book is just an object with a certain size and weight—an object to transport from Point A to Point B without any damage. In this way, what's important about a thing can be completely different from a different vantage point.

Viewing things from multiple angles means looking at them from the perspectives of many different people. When you think about something from someone else's perspective, you can see new sides to it. You might find the seeds of a new idea or discover a hidden trap.

From my perspective as the writer, I'm most likely to fall into the trap of thinking people will buy the book based on the quality of the content. From the book designer's viewpoint, however, no matter how good the content is, if people in bookstores don't pick up the book in the first place, it won't sell well. So, from the designer's perspective, the "pop" of the cover design and the look of the interior pages are crucial. For the people working at the bookstore, the content and design are important, but they might also think a low price is vital for the book to sell well. Readers, meanwhile, might think completely different things are important.

The list goes on. Sellers, buyers, operators of the platform, sales consultants, developers... Depending on our vantage point, we will all view the same product completely differently. Always remember that there's no single correct way of looking at the world.

The world is built on subjectivity, and there is some genuine validity to every subjective view. The same thing won't necessarily look the same to the person right next to you. Never try to view the world exclusively from your own perspective but make a habit of imagining how other people might view things and how they might feel about them.

An eye that sees things from many diverse perspectives is a powerful weapon in business. Seeing from every angle provides you with insights the competition may miss. That can be a powerful competitive edge.

61 Keep your eyes on what's at your feet and what lies ahead

We all have our strong points and weak points—things at which we excel and others at which we don't.

In skiing, some of us will keep our eyes on the ground under our feet, while some of us will only look into the distance. If you look closely, you'll see that skiers who do both with just the right balance are rare.

If you're always looking down, you'll lose sight of where you are going. And if you're always looking off into the distance, you'll lose your balance and fall over. Likewise, in business, it's important to maintain a good balance between tasks close at hand and the objectives far in the distance.

To develop this balance for yourself, first you need to understand what type of person you are. Are you the type with your eyes on the ground at your feet, or are you looking to future goals?

If you have big dreams, but tend to run into problems or make mistakes at work, then you're the type who always looks too far ahead. If you give your all to your daily tasks but gain a reputation for only being able to do the work that's given to you, you're the teammate who is looking down at the ground—too grounded in the present.

Once you know which type of person you are, you should compensate for your weak points.

If you are the type with your eyes on the ground beneath you, then you should try thinking about the meaning of the work you're doing within the overall scheme of things. If you can't figure it out yourself, ask others around you for their opinions.

If you are the type always looking far into the future, you should focus on the tasks at hand now and concentrate on doing them well. Remember that doing your current task well is the first step toward realizing your dreams for the future.

The expression "can't see the forest for the trees" exists because so many of us become fixated with the ground beneath us and forget to look at the big picture. Despite this, I think the opposite is also true—especially in the business world in recent times. A surprisingly large number of people can't see the trees for the forest—and it seems many of them can be found in the internet business. I wouldn't go so far as to label them all dreamers, but the fact is that the world is now changing so rapidly that unless you're also keeping an eye on the ground at your feet and adapting accordingly, the likelihood of failure is high.

Sure, it's vital to draw up business plans focused on the future. But if that's all you do, your business will quickly become disconnected from the present reality. No matter how accurate your forecast may ultimately prove to be, if you're not delivering on your day-to-day tasks, you are not going to succeed. Ultimately, the essence of work comes down almost entirely to how proficiently you deliver on everyday tasks. It's only after you've become proficient at everyday tasks that the ability to predict the future even starts to become valuable.

Keep up your daily efforts and the future will be yours. See the trees and see the forest; develop the ability to see both clearly.

62 Factorize

I've written that whatever the goal, there's practically no target that can't be achieved. I can make this assertion because no matter what the objective, it is capable of being factorized—like a mathematical equation. Everything is made up of many integral elements.

Long ago, it was said that a journey of 1,000 miles begins with a single step. No matter how confident you might be, you would certainly flinch if you were suddenly told that your next target was to walk 1,000 miles. But a single step? Anyone can do that. Keep on doing that and you'll surely be able to make even 1,000 miles.

Set goals, then break down the path to those goals into the smallest unit—single steps. This is the only way you can be certain to achieve your targets.

This is not a simple process. I use the term *factorize* because there are many business targets that can be simplified by dividing them up with parentheses. Remember that if you thoroughly break down even your seemingly impossible goals into smaller, more manageable units, they will become achievable.

Factorization makes even complex mathematical equations simple and easy to understand.

Business goals are the same. It may seem at first glance that a multitude of tasks must be done to reach them. But if you think through these calmly, as you would factorize an equation, you'll be able to break down the necessary tasks into a number of simple elements.

What's important here is the thoroughness of your factorization. Half-measures are no good. If you leave unknowns in the calculation, you won't be able to map out your route to success.

Reverse engineering of competitors' products, commonplace in the fields of automotive and electronics manufacturing, is a form of factorization. Companies take new competitor products apart, right down to the smallest screw, and thoroughly analyze them, studying their entire structure. Regardless of how revolutionary the product, it's easy to reproduce if you analyze it this extensively. However complex a machine may be, it's still just the sum of its parts.

Of course, companies don't reverse engineer products to simply recreate them. They do it to develop better products. It's the same when thinking about what you need to do to achieve your goals.

To achieve goals, you must first break them down. If you can do that, you'll understand the true nature of the task at hand.

Among all the various elements that contribute to achieving a goal, the key thing is that no matter what the goal, there is no way of achieving it other than to take the steps you can right here and now.

This is the way I encouraged my employees to approach English language learning. When I announced the company would adopt English as its primary language, there was naturally quite a lot of concern. Many feared they would be unable to do their jobs in English. What would that mean for their careers? How would they survive? How could they learn English overnight?

So I was quick to explain that I had no expectations this would happen overnight. Only that the first steps be taken overnight. It took many steps to get this company to my goal of Englishnization. It took years. It took many changes and iterations to the original plan. But by breaking it down into achievable small steps, we as a company were able to make the long stride into a new language. We are now a showcase for how an entire company can adapt to the globalized business world through language learning. That did not happen in one big step; it was the sum of many small ones.

What exactly do you need to do right now? Find that out by factorizing thoroughly, and then you can give it your all.

63 Lean operations generate innovation and growth

Ants are thought to be hard workers, but I've heard that if you look closely you'll find that it's only a few of the ants that are actually working. The majority wander around achieving very little.

The business world and the ants have much in common. That's not to say that if you look closely you'll find most people are wandering around aimlessly. Most of us will seem to be busy. But much of this busyness is going to waste. Think about your own job. Most of what you do goes to waste. What proportion that is depends on you and your company, but this problem is a constant. So if you can reduce any waste in business, you are directly enabling growth. This is a key to making any business soar.

However, this is not a simple surface effort of cutting costs to increase profitability. If you start talking about cutting costs, many people will think you are going to sacrifice growth. This is seen as a choice about whether or not to invest in growth.

This way of thinking is completely wrong.

Cost-cutting is to a company what a proper diet and strength training are to an athlete. It's meant to trim fat and build muscle. Unnecessary costs in business are like fat. It's much easier to move dynamically if you trim away the fat and build up muscle.

In business, if you reduce waste, it becomes easier to innovate. It becomes easier to develop new products and generate new services. By no means is cost cutting a negative, but rather, it's a positive for an organization when conducted with purpose.

For example, say 10 people are doing a job. If you told one person to take on that whole job alone, they'd probably say it's impossible. But in my experience, this is always going to be possible—because when individuals take it upon themselves to do something, they almost always succeed.

Or, if I'm in a meeting and I'm told that a certain goal is estimated to take three months to accomplish, my response is to ask to get it done in 10 days. People used to get annoyed with this response—even though I'm the CEO of the company—and tell me my demands were unreasonable. But they've stopped saying that nowadays, because people almost always manage to meet the deadlines. Of course, this is going to be difficult if you're resorting to your usual old work habits. If you use your head and innovate, then it becomes possible. I have developed a number of speed "hacks" over the years that I apply routinely to cut waste. One is the tactic I just described—whatever the deadline is, I cut it. Everyone moves faster with a deadline looming. I also do small things such as insisting on stand-up meetings (no one drones on when everyone is standing). I invest in amenities such as a free cafeteria and a modern gym at my headquarters so that employees will not have to spend precious hours traveling to lunch or a workout. These are only small things, but they add up and make us all more efficient.

Rakuten has employed such methods for over 20 years. People often tell me that making further efficiency gains will be difficult. However, somehow there's always a way. It seems to be in the nature of organizations to generate waste.

Running a lean operation means eliminating waste and making operations as simple as possible. Don't eliminate just a little of the waste. Cut it all out. If things can be done in parallel, do them simultaneously. If single operations can be made to serve multiple functions, make sure all of those functions are achieved. Do all this thoroughly. A thousand miles in geographical terms is always a thousand miles, but in business, innovation can reduce a distance of a thousand miles into a hundred, or even ten. Use that to radically reduce the time it takes you to achieve your goals, or dramatically reduce the number of people assigned to a project. To achieve goals in that short time period with so few people, you will have to radically eliminate waste as well. This will generate breakthroughs and drive your personal and organizational growth.

64 Think about both vertical and horizontal competition

Vertical competition may well be an entirely modern phenomenon. Previously, competition nearly always meant horizontal competition. Ramen Restaurant A opens next to Ramen Restaurant B. This is a textbook example of horizontal competition.

But then perhaps their noodle supplier opens a mail-order business so anyone can enjoy the same delicious ramen at home. All of a sudden, the noodle maker who they had never thought of as a competitor is in direct competition with the ramen restaurants. This is a textbook example of vertical competition.

In this way, some industries that no one ever thought would be in direct competition are fighting for the same market.

Some say that comic books lost popularity because of the rise of video games. They both competed for children's free time. Today, the internet and mobile phones are also competing for attention. The competitors in the ring evolve and change surprisingly quickly.

Right now, TV companies see internet-based entertainment as a competitor, but this situation could change at any moment. Maybe electronics manufacturers will be their next competitors? And for internet-related companies like Rakuten, the possibilities to begin competing in other industries are almost endless.

For internet companies in particular, technological innovation happens at extremely high speeds. Companies in entirely different business areas today could be your competitors tomorrow. I expect WhatsApp did not consider an e-commerce platform like Rakuten Ichiba a direct competitor until we purchased Viber and entered the messaging space. Airlines once competing only in the travel industry are now competitors to our cashback shopping platform Ebates, as they expand their points and loyalty efforts. Nothing in the internet business is ever fixed—and that includes your roster of rivals.

I've been thinking about how to defend against this phenomenon since I started Rakuten. Thinking about this may be the fate of all companies involved in internet businesses.

The following is true, not just for the internet business, but other companies, too: These days, every business must think constantly about what kind of business might replace the service it provides. It also has to think about which areas it can move into. There is no longer such a thing as a fixed, constant way to approach your business.

Of course, simply competing is not the way to win. You can also improve your position by aligning yourself with companies in other industries. I wouldn't go so far as to compare business today to the violent and tumultuous Sengoku Period—an era primarily in the sixteenth century marked by social upheaval and military conflict—but it is worth remembering that your enemy today may be your ally tomorrow.

Obviously, it's better if you can transition from a rivalry to a relationship in which both sides benefit. To this end, you must always think about horizontal and vertical competition. The keys to surviving the Sengoku Period of today are a flexible mind, versatile thinking, and a grand vision. This is what makes business today so fascinating.

65 The Mikitani Curve: Quality depends on a 0.5 percent difference in effort

Any competitive society is premised on the notion that everyone will work hard. Whether it's televisions, cars, or rice cookers, manufacturers will do their utmost to make products of the highest possible quality. The same is true for commerce—your local café, restaurants, and Rakuten Ichiba stores. Everyone will work as hard as possible to hone his or her skills and provide the best possible product or service.

And yet, obvious differences exist in the quality of certain products and services. Why? How do these differences arise?

I think it's all about the last half-percent of extra effort that went into their creation.

Anyone can strive to work as hard as possible. But, after they've done their best, can they do half a percent more? This is where the difference lies.

You may have completed a task and think you're finished, but you must not stop there. Spend a bit more time on it. You probably won't be able to add very much—because you think everything that can be done has been already. Nevertheless, don't be satisfied with that. Add something. Even if it's only a half percent. Even tiny differences, even going 0.5 percent over the top, will make a big difference. Your customers will notice.

Say you have a piece of cotton and a piece of silk. Which feels smoother? You can tell immediately by feeling them. However, if you examine the surfaces, they probably differ by less than 0.1 mm. Pieces of silk and cotton clearly differ in quality, but even some silk differs from other silk, cotton from other cotton. Expressed in numbers, the difference can be practically zero. But even so, people will notice that different feel, that smoothness—differences that might even be invisible to a machine. And an almost insignificant difference can mean a huge difference in price.

Nevertheless, very few people think about this when they do their job. Hence, that 0.5 percent becomes a very large difference. This is what I mean when I say "the last step is always the most important." It's the difference made by an extra 0.5 percent of effort. Always be aware of this decisive difference, and create systems to ensure you continue to make this final 0.5 percent effort. This final step rapidly improves the subjective quality of a product, generating a new growth trajectory (I call it the Mikitani Curve). It determines not only products and services, but also the value of people.

Ordinary people and outstanding people: the difference between them also depends on the last 0.5 percent of effort.

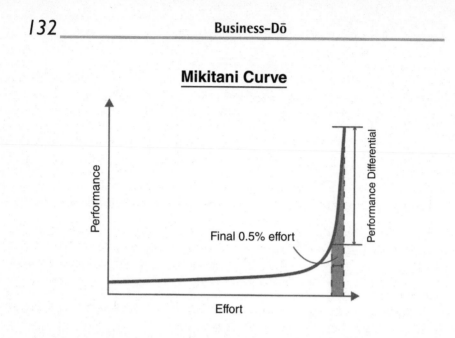

Mikitani Curve

66 Identify what is core and what is mission-critical

When a company becomes large, the different types of businesses it operates also seem to naturally multiply. In turn, this raises resource allocation issues, but, no matter how big a company becomes, resources are always going to have limits. In order to effectively allocate your finite resources, the ability to identify and shut down nonessential businesses is crucial.

Making this judgment is surprisingly difficult. For many companies, this problem is often the reason behind a decline in earnings or bad performance. Managers of businesses can be as emotional and stubborn as anyone. So that my judgment isn't clouded by such emotions, I've defined three key criteria for the survival of a business. If a business doesn't meet any of these three criteria, that's clearly the time to shut it down.

The first is high profitability. This probably goes without saying: If something's profitable, keep doing it. If it's not, don't. This is a fairly obvious assessment to make in business. In fact, if this was the only factor, the assessment would be easy, but a company won't survive long-term if it's focused only on profitability. Companies are living things. If you ate nothing but carbohydrates because they are a great source of energy, eventually you would get sick. You also need protein and calcium to build muscles and bones.

This leads me to my second point: Is the business a core business? A core business is one that is a company's bread and butter, or part of its identity. You might even say it represents the company's reason for being. In many cases, it will be the business that a company first started out in, but not necessarily so. It's a core business that will sustain a company in the long term.

The third point has to do with being mission-critical or not. Just as vitamins and minerals are not a source of energy but essential nevertheless, mission-critical operations are those that are essential for a company's survival. In Rakuten's case, our membership program is an example of this. It may not generate profit, but it is clearly very important to Rakuten as a whole. Similarly, our baseball team is mission-critical to our marketing strategy.

These three criteria act as the basis for my decisions on whether to continue with a business. If a business meets one of these criteria, I look for some way of continuing it, even if it's not going well now. But if it doesn't meet any one of the three, I will make the decision to discontinue it, no matter how difficult that may be. The important thing is not to continue the business simply for the sake of it, but to do so based on solid grounds and standards.

Shutting a business down can be painful, but it's the same as pruning a tree. Leaving all the branches to grow at random can hinder the growth of the most important branches. I've heard that when left unpruned, trees are more likely to fall victim to pests and disease. Companies are living things, too, and face similar problems.

Determining criteria like this can be helpful not only in business, but also when thinking about your own personal plans and activities. What are your own core businesses and what is mission-critical? How can you boost your profits? Take the time to pause and consider these criteria. Are you spending time on wasteful "businesses" that don't meet any of these criteria, at the expense of something more important?

67 Deciding not to do something can be the most important thing to do

When people make plans, we first think about what we'll do. We don't usually think about what we won't do. It's easy to decide what you will do, but difficult to decide on what you won't do. This is because deciding not to do something is abandoning a possibility. Even if you don't actually do something, as long as you don't decide not to do it, the possibility remains. We want to hold onto all these possibilities and so we hold back from making a decision against doing something until the very last moment.

However, there are certain times and situations when deciding not to do something will yield a far better result. A straightforward example is the decision to shut down a business. Shutting down a business means abandoning the possibility of winning beyond that point. None of us wants to do that, so we put off the decision, and the damage grows. If you're going to shut something down, the sooner the better and, accordingly, the less the damage.

Determining the victor and the loser is difficult enough on the battlefield but perhaps even harder in business. But however hard this may be, it remains the case that delaying this call will only amplify the damage.

If you're not sure of your ability to determine whether you've won or lost, then you should draw up your own criteria for making this assessment. Your criteria might include market share or profitability, depending on the type of business or the competitive environment. But no matter what criteria you use, the best ones are objective, clear criteria, and, if possible, criteria that can be expressed in numbers. We can't help but become emotional when we're losing and emotion clouds our judgment. You can minimize this if you use numbers to provide an objective standard. You should think of the decision to shut down as another effort—to minimize the damage caused by the loss of a battle.

This approach isn't just effective when shutting something down. Deciding not to do something prevents future loss and waste. We made a series of difficult decisions in 2016 to pull our e-commerce marketplace businesses out of markets including the United Kingdom, Spain, and Indonesia. But, at the same time, we continue to invest in these very same countries—in new models that offer more potential for growth, like ridesharing and fintech.

When I founded Rakuten, it was at the end of an exploratory process I conducted in which I considered—and rejected— more than one other possible industry for my new business. When a company is growing, there are many temptations. And once you've established a comfortable level of capital, you may be tempted to venture into another highly profitable business. Even if I don't think this myself, someone in the company will inevitably bring it up.

If you haven't decided against doing something, when someone brings up the possibility, you'll have to spend time discussing it and making that decision. And sometimes the act of discussing a possible idea can interfere with the core business of your company. Core businesses are important to preserve a company's identity, but deciding what not to do is also crucial in order to stay true to the company's core mission.

68 Companies are sumo rings. They need wrestlers

With Japan's lifetime employment system disappearing over time, it's no longer uncommon for people to change jobs to get ahead in their careers. Employees who believe in putting their company ahead of everything else, including themselves, are quickly becoming relics of a bygone era. Even so, the way employees think about companies is still basically the same.

What is a company? Some might suggest it's the property of its shareholders. That's one way to look at it. But for employees, that's not always a helpful definition. After all, management bears responsibilities toward the shareholders, but this doesn't mean employees must work for them, too.

Arguments about who really owns a company are essentially nonsense. Because a company is not a physical thing: Without the people working there, a company really isn't anything at all. It's not as if investors risk their capital just to admire a company's buildings and facilities.

I believe a company is a group of people with a shared vision and common aspirations. My ideal company is a place where people come together freely, having decided to advance toward a common goal in order to realize that vision and achieve those aspirations. That said, it's meaningless unless every single one of those people can also achieve happiness. And of course, making a profit must also never be forgotten as part of the equation.

The company is the arena: Just like a sumo ring. The main event isn't the ring itself, but rather, the sumo wrestlers who are in the ring, or the company's employees.

Never for a moment forget that no matter who owns the sumo ring, you and your fellow employees are the key players in the main event.

69 Master the timeline

In business, it's vital to see the big picture, and that big picture must also include the element of time. While the saying goes, "You can't see the forest for the trees," the truth is you have to see both the trees and the forest, as well as be able to predict how the forest will change, and prepare for that. It's not enough to just analyze the present circumstances. You must also forecast future change.

My biggest concern is that so many of us are so slow to take action. I often look at a situation and wonder why it is only being addressed now, when the current circumstances were clearly and easily foreseeable. In so many cases, if there had been some forecasting of future circumstances and some basic and necessary preparations made, the issues would have been resolved long ago.

In business, being the first to move gives you many advantages over the late-starter. Unlike games like "Go" or chess, you don't need to take turns to make a move in business. You can make multiple moves at once, and sometimes you can even put your opponent into check before they've begun.

That said, it's not always the case that doing everything early is best. There are times when it's better just to make preparations and wait for the right time, rather than act immediately. No matter how advantageous it may seem to make the first move, you can't harvest the fruit before it's ripe.

That's why you must take into account the element of time. To put it simply, you should anticipate the passage of things to come and do what's necessary when the time is right. Conceived in Japan, Rakuten is now worldwide, but that did not happen overnight. We grew and expanded in stages.

People sometimes talk about applying stage theory to management. Whether it's about people or companies, it's vital to understand objectively what stage you're at and implement appropriate plans. Depending on the stage, there are times when you will be solely focused on going after profit growth and there will also be times when you'll want to sacrifice some profits to promote expansion.

What you should do will depend on the stage you're at. What stage are you at right now? And what should you do at this stage? Just like looking at a map, you must take into account the element of time as part of the big picture and make your decision based on that. Developing this ability is crucial in business.

70 The devil is in the details

In Japan, you're more likely to hear the phrase "God is in the details."

So which is it really? God or the devil? It fascinates me personally that the English and Japanese languages are so diametrically opposed on this point. Thinking God is in the details suits Japan, since my home country enjoys seeing small things done well. Japanese automakers took the world by storm because of the care they took to ensure that even the smallest components of each car were perfect. As an example, thorough quality control radically minimized the number of poor quality parts. This focus on detail enabled Japanese automakers to overtake US manufacturers.

From the Japanese perspective, God is in the smallest detail. From the English-speaking perspective, the more common rendition of that expression is: The devil is in the details. Paying close attention to detail generates opportunities in the Japanese language, while, in English, ignoring them could lead you into a devil's trap.

In essence, both of these phrases mean the same thing. No matter how valid the idea behind a business model may be, if the details aren't right, it will often fail. This kind of failure is a terrible waste: to start a new business and simply give up if things don't go well. When this happens, we must consider whether the problem was with the business model itself or the details of its implementation.

If the problem is in the details, it isn't difficult to fix. Giving everything up just because it doesn't go well at first is a hasty choice. There are many cases where businesses that have done well end in failure because of a lack of attention to the detail. I would say that the cause of the great majority of failures comes down to problems in the details.

When I talk about problems in the details, I'm basically talking about the way businesses are executed and operated. You can call these procedural issues. No matter how outstanding the business model, it won't succeed if there are problems with the way procedures are executed in practice. Here's an example: No matter how good your product is, it won't sell if the salesperson doesn't feel motivated. This problem arises frequently in actual business. It's a detail of execution—an element that can be overlooked by the team launching the business—and it can derail the whole project.

When you look at it this way, it might really be that the devil is the one hidden in the details.

71 Success is born of failure. Never hesitate to improve

Just because you failed, there's no point in brooding. Failures help you to identify problems. Once you know where a problem lies, all you have to do is solve it.

By failing, you're also discovering things you should improve, and if you make these improvements, you can be sure of making progress. So when you fail, rather than sulking about it, you should get excited.

But also be sure to make the improvements immediately. "Success is born of failure." The wisdom of this old Japanese proverb only comes to life if you have the discipline to make improvements following that failure. When problems are revealed, be quick to remedy them. By being faithful to this principle, both individuals and companies can make progress.

Failure only ends in failure when it isn't used to spur improvements. And this only happens because of a lack of quick action—if you don't get to work on improvements straight away, you're bound to repeat the same mistake. Some people will make the same mistake over and over again. They will spend their lives always stumbling on the same stone, no matter how many times they come across it.

Another way to think about failure is this: The things you fail at are things other people would likely fail at as well. Conversely, this means the things you fail at also hold hidden opportunities. By succeeding in the place where others have failed, you will be that much further ahead of the pack. Failure therefore contains a hidden key to major progress.

When you trip over a rock, take a good look at it. It might be a precious stone.

72 Find trends in the numbers

Sales, profit margin, break-even point, ordinary profit, market share, customer spend, store traffic—these are just a few of the many metrics you'll encounter in business. Being good with numbers is crucial to being a manager. Numbers are facts: They don't lie. To give you an objective picture of both the overall performance and details of a business, nothing is more reliable than the numbers.

But if I go so far as to say that, some will make the counter-argument that sometimes numbers do in fact lie. For example, a shady investment business will use all sorts of impressive graphs and calculations to tell their story but, no matter how good the story, the numbers will be full of lies.

So there are instances out there like that, but this is also precisely why you need to be good with numbers.

Numbers only tell lies if they're misinterpreted. With the exception of deliberately falsified data, people are usually misled by numbers because they misread them.

To read numbers correctly, you need to develop the ability to connect them to reality. You could call this the ability to extrapolate from the numbers, and imagine something bigger. If you don't have this skill, just being fast at calculations or good at memorizing numbers will be of no use to you in business. Conversely, if you do, reading the numbers becomes fun.

Some baseball fans are incredibly knowledgeable about baseball player stats. This is probably the same quality. Just by looking at the numbers, they can visualize how a player has played. That's why figures that are dry as dust to some are incredibly interesting to others.

Monitoring changes in numerical data is a good way of building your skill in reading the numbers.

Rakuten employees send daily reports to their managers. In our early days, this came in the form of paper memos, and just one day's data amounts to a stack of paper at least five centimeters thick. While this is a large pile of data, by carefully reading through the figures every day, I started seeing various things. For example, I became able to discern whether a change in the numbers was an issue I needed to pay attention to or not. I could tell if any one section's profits were trending up or down.

I look at the numbers in my business and in my wider industry every day, and these numbers often make clear what we must do next. When we could see the numbers showing the rise in mobile app usage, we were naturally inspired to create a Rakuten shopping app. When numbers revealed a jump in the use of messaging apps, that was a key factor in our decision to acquire Viber. I also use the numbers as a personnel tool. When I look at the daily numbers from my company, I can often see immediately who needs my attention and who is doing just fine without my hovering. This makes me more efficient as a manager and I'm sure makes it easier for my managers to do their jobs—knowing I will be hands on or hands off in their daily workings, as the numbers dictate.

Just by looking at numbers you can see not only what's happening in your business, but also to some extent what's going on in the world at large. There are countless examples of business ideas and opportunities for improvement that have been revealed in this way.

73 Think about value chains

A value chain is a series of steps that create value. The idea for Rakuten Ichiba was premised on my belief that the internet was going to spread like wildfire. Actually, I'd considered several other internet business models, but Rakuten Ichiba—an internet shopping mall—was the one I settled on, because it was clearly much more likely to create a value chain than any of the others.

Rakuten Ichiba is like a stage, or an empty space. On its own, it has no value. What creates the value are the stores in that space. There are two types of value. One is value for the merchants. If you open a store on Rakuten Ichiba, you can sell your products. This is the value created by opening a store on the site. The other type is value for the end user, the people who shop on the site. If they go to Rakuten Ichiba, they can find all kinds of things for sale. It therefore also has value for shoppers. These two types of value create a chain reaction.

I noted earlier that when Rakuten Ichiba opened in 1997 it had only 13 stores. Frankly, it didn't have much of either type of value to begin with. From an end-user perspective, the product offering was sparse and, from the merchants' perspective, there were too few shoppers to drive product sales.

As I've noted, I set a low opening fee, even though I was aware we might incur losses, so that merchants wouldn't be burdened by weak sales. There would be value in having a store on the site even if sellers made only a modest profit. Then the six of us rushed around Japan drumming up business.

It was hard, but we managed to sign up 100 merchants in the first year. In the second, we signed up 200. In the third, the number of stores were increasing by 100 every month. As the number of stores increased, so did the number of shoppers on the site. As the number of shoppers increased, so did the number of stores—the two types of value created a chain reaction. Unlike in an ordinary business, the more we sell, the greater Rakuten Ichiba's value and appeal becomes for both merchants and customers.

There are currently more than 44,000 merchants on Rakuten Ichiba. While we have yet to reach our limit, the population of Japan is finite. The number of shops is no longer rising exponentially. For those who open stores on the site, the increase in the number of merchants also means the advent of competition. However, this competition drives the creation of new value and the appeal of Rakuten Ichiba. There is direct competition, specifically price competition, but merchants also compete to improve the quality of their products. They try new strategies like offering products not available elsewhere, improving their service levels and building relationships of trust with their customers. The efforts of the merchants to improve make Rakuten Ichiba more diverse and improve the quality of the site.

A value chain can be a strong asset. Think about the values in your own business, and how to link them effectively. This is something that can be applied to any business.

74 To win, close the gaps and add originality

How wide are the gaps between you and your competitors?

Considering this will help you to win against the rivals that are out there ahead of you.

In the restaurant business, for example, they might be ahead of you in terms of the tastiness of the food, the service, the value for money, or the atmosphere. In any one of a number of areas, you will be able to identify gaps in your performance, so work to understand those and close the gaps. In other words, completely eliminate any gaps between your performance and those of your rivals. Fill in those gaps.

Once you've done that, then work to add in something original. The results of that equation will put you ahead. This is the kind of arithmetic that grade-schoolers can understand. But it's something that surprisingly few of us get done.

We tend to think that we can't beat rivals by copying them, and focus only on developing an original approach, striving to make something unique—and failing as a result.

Competitors win because they have something original, but working to close the gaps between you and them will allow you to neutralize the effect of their originality. Once you've achieved that, from the customer perspective, the restaurants will be equal. If you then add your own original touch, it becomes clear who will win.

In the manufacturing world, this process is called *reverse engineering*. Companies will take apart a competitor's finished product in order to thoroughly understand every aspect of how it works. It's called reverse engineering because it's the reverse of the usual development process. By taking the product apart, you understand exactly what differentiates it from your product. Then, once you eliminate these disparities, the gap between you and your competitor disappears. Close the gaps, then add originality, and you will come out ahead.

Your originality will only count once you've eliminated the gaps between you and your competitors.

75 No business is special

It has been said that every industry has its own unique challenges, that manufacturing and services operate differently, and even businesses in the same industry, such as soba restaurants and ramen bars, face different issues.

It's this kind of thinking that leads to business failure.

There will always be some distinguishing features of a business, but these are only ever on the surface, because the fundamental logic of business hardly ever changes. When people insist on seeing one business as completely different from another, that just serves to prove that they're only seeing the surface and don't understand the fundamental logic. They will find business difficult and, ultimately, almost always fail.

A ramen bar and a high-class French restaurant might seem to be completely different. But the fundamentals of successful restaurants are really very similar: the attitude of staff toward their jobs, the effort put into each dish, the efficiency of the kitchen, the looks of satisfaction on customers' faces as they leave. There are no differences on these counts.

The profit equation, of sales minus costs, holds true for all businesses. Usually, there's an inverse relationship between increasing sales and reducing costs. That's the commonality between all businesses that is so difficult, and why the same things are important in every business. To boost sales, you must first increase customer satisfaction. Sales not based on customer satisfaction are like morning dew: They evaporate as the sun comes up.

Customer satisfaction is the value of the satisfaction derived from the purchase by the customer, minus the cost of the purchase. If the outcome of this equation is negative, the customer is not likely to buy anything from you ever again. The result of the sum needs to be at least zero, if not positive. For successful stores, this result will be far more positive than that of competitors. What makes a customer satisfied depends on why they came to the store in the first place. So we must think deeply to understand what is driving the customer and how much effort we should make to ensure their satisfaction. Or, in other words, how far should you boost the added value offered by your products or services? This fundamental logic never changes.

Of course, if you want to increase profit, it's also important to reduce costs, but if that's all you do, customer satisfaction will swiftly decline. Managers who understand this strive as far as possible to reduce waste and boost cost-effectiveness. Popular ramen bars and French restaurants are fundamentally alike because there aren't many different ways of achieving this. It basically hinges on staff quality. This is the same for any business.

These fundamental factors don't change, whether it be a business in the food and beverage industry, finance, the environmental industry, or even the biomedical industry. Nor do the fundamental principles of marketing or sales. Whatever the sector, the same basic principles apply.

Rakuten has been successful because we've treated the internet business like any other business. Even the business of professional baseball is the same as any other business; that's why our professional baseball business has also been so successful.

No business is special. When you encounter new difficulties, always come back to this principle.

76 Boost profits by using assets in multiple ways

There is no need to leave your assets idle.

Companies have a wide variety of resources: Multipurpose use means using those resources for multiple purposes to drive higher profit. A simple example of using resources in multiple ways is a café that turns into a bar at night.

For Rakuten, our servers are a resource, as are the software programs and other technology used by Rakuten Ichiba and other Rakuten businesses. We could go so far as to say our customer base is also a major resource.

Such resources may normally only be used for a single purpose but we must always examine them carefully from many different angles and consider whether there aren't other ways of using them.

In farming, one field can produce two crops in the same year—say, rice and wheat, a process known as *double cropping*. This concept is also applicable to business.

The café that turns into a bar at night is an example of multipurpose use of resources. Another is an entertainment product that might run in theaters, on TV, and online. Some companies have started to make multipurpose use of their office PCs. In most businesses, employees turn off their PCs when they finish work, but in these companies, the PCs are left on. By keeping the computers running at night, depending on how many can be hooked up to each other, they can perform calculations nearly on a par with a supercomputer. This eliminates the need for a true supercomputer. This is another example of using a resource in multiple ways—in this case, PCs.

With multipurpose use of resources, you can substantially reduce operating expenses. Generally speaking, using resources like this generates hardly any additional cost, so you can significantly increase profitability. If you pass these savings on to customers, their satisfaction will increase, and this will boost profits even further.

At Rakuten, we're also striving to leverage our customer base in multiple ways. Skilled utilization of *intangible assets* has a big impact on profitability. This is what the concept at the core of the Rakuten Ecosystem represents. If Rakuten Ichiba customers also begin to use Rakuten Travel or Rakuten Securities, our costs are dramatically reduced, as we almost take out altogether the cost of customer acquisition, a high proportion of our overall costs. And by passing these savings on to our customers, we can attract even more customers. Almost any kind of economic activity is possible within the Rakuten Group, and by bringing benefits to our customers, we begin to create a total ecosystem. This is another example of making multiple uses of our customer base as a resource.

I predict that resources that can't be used in multiple ways—in other words, resources with poor utilization rates—will be discarded. If a business isn't making any money, it's usually due to poor utilization of resources.

77 Strategy, execution, and operation

Strategy, execution, operation. All businesses develop via a cycle of these three steps: you draw up a strategy, work out the details of how to execute it, then launch operations. Businesses grow by repeating this process.

The main problem here, however, is that many of us put too much emphasis on strategy.

There is a commonly held misperception that success depends entirely on strategy. Stories of legendary people and their successes are all about the strategy, probably because it sounds far more impressive than the other two elements of success, and it's easier to explain. Japanese military history typifies this approach. Minamoto Yoshitsune is a twelfth-century Japanese military leader acclaimed for coming up with a strategy to split his forces and attack his enemy from both the front and rear of its position. Toyotomi Hideyoshi was a samurai known for ordering the construction Sunomata Castle in a single night—a move designed to intimidate his enemy. From my perspective, many of these legends are nine-tenths fiction.

But even if they weren't, I think the execution of these plans offers far more insight than the strategy. How did Yoshitsune get his horses down a steep cliff for that rear assault? And what building process got Sunomata up overnight? The strategies are interesting, but what I want to know is: How?

Of course, military histories don't go into all of these things. Even if they did, they would be so boring, no one would read them. But these boring details matter if you want to achieve something.

The same thing crops up in business. Once failure is recognized, there is very little effort made to determine at which stage of the cycle the cause of failure lies. It is surprisingly common to see people jump to the conclusion that failure was due to a faulty strategy or business model.

Faulty business model = failure. Expressed as an equation like this, it looks convincing. But I believe that the exact opposite is true. Most failures are not the result of a faulty strategy but of issues with execution and operation. The strategy isn't wrong. The causes of failure are much more likely to lie in implementation.

When I first started working on my ideas for online shopping, many people said the business model had already been proven flawed. At the time, several major companies were already operating such malls and weren't doing well.

However, I believed the problem wasn't the business model, but something else. I took a look at other sites and was not impressed. They were slow to update and a lot of the information on display was old. You could find a site advertising Christmas goods just days before Valentine's Day.

Companies running internet shopping mall sites at that time were creating website pages on behalf of each of the stores selling goods on their sites. You had to be a technical expert to make changes to the sites because the sites were so difficult to use. As a result, swapping out just one product picture took a lot of time and effort. The internet's strength lies in the speed at which it can deliver information, but no one was taking advantage of that.

This wasn't a flaw in the business model. The problem lay in the execution. At Rakuten, we solved this problem by developing a system that allowed store owners to create their own simple web pages. Although we were amateurs, we took on the challenge of developing a unique system that was not to be found anywhere else at the time. It wouldn't have been unreasonable to label it impossible at the time, but if we'd failed, obviously Rakuten wouldn't exist today.

It's important to think about strategy, but never forget the importance of execution and operation. There's a huge scope for creativity in these two areas as well. How much thought and energy will you invest in this? This will make all the difference to whether or not you can make the impossible possible and achieve a dream.

78 No single path leads to success

There are as many paths to success as there are people trying to achieve it. Even when you're headed toward the same goal, there is no need to take the same path as those who have gone before you.

When you climb a mountain and find a path, it's natural to want to take it. It feels like the best way to get to the summit. In business, however, this is a foolish idea. Because no matter how fast you climb, someone is already ahead of you, obstructing that path. The path to success in business is narrow, like an animal trail. Think of it as only being wide enough for one person. It's not impossible to overtake others on the same route, but it's extremely difficult. In order to overtake your rivals, it's better to seek out a new path.

You should create your own path in business. There isn't just one route to the top. There are always other approaches that no one else has tried.

Take Google's search engine. Everyone already seems to have concluded that it's unbeatable but it could be possible to build a system based on a completely different approach that would far surpass Google. Nonetheless, few have tried to do so. This is probably because somewhere deep down we are all thinking that there might only be one path to success.

On another note, there's a second lesson to be drawn from this principle: that when someone succeeds at something, they try to repeat their success. In other words, they insist on going after the same winning pattern.

A pattern is a type of framework that, of course, can be applied in other competitive situations. So there's nothing wrong with having a winning formula—as I've written in another section, if you establish a winning formula you can apply it in other fields. However, it's dangerous if you always insist on it. Your winning formula isn't everything—you must never forget that.

There is no single path to success. If you don't always keep this principle in your mind, you will lose your ability to think flexibly and end up trapped in the same pattern over and over again.

79 Generate the largest cost advantage to win

Mention cost cutting and discussions will quickly turn to scaling back operations and abandoning plans but this is the wrong approach. First, cutting costs is a creative job on par with drawing up a new business model. Second, cost cutting is not an obstacle to growth. To the contrary, you should cut costs in order to accelerate growth.

We've started doing this at Rakuten, and we've succeeded in significantly reducing costs. Naturally, we've made structural change in our tech development division and substantially reduced corporate spending. One good example is an initiative to halve the number of meetings, the number of participants in meetings, and the time spent in meetings. This makes a half cubed, so we reduced the cost of meetings down to one eighth. This approach isn't limited to meetings. In principle, it can be applied to all work. We can halve the number of redundant tasks. We can halve the number of people assigned to a particular task. We can halve the amount of time spent on a task. They say time is money, but in a company, time and costs have equal value.

Of course, these weren't the only things we did. The substantial cut in annual costs was due to our efforts to sharply reduce waste even in small things, such as printing on both sides of paper and shrinking text when making copies. We even made the use of our office elevators more efficient.

We would not have been able to achieve this if we had set more modest targets. Aiming for a 5 percent or 10 percent cost reduction would have been pointless. It's precisely because we aimed for reductions of a half to a third that our efforts were effective. To reduce costs that much you have to fundamentally change the way you do business.

For example, when a company enters a new field, it is likely to strive to invest as much as possible in the initiative. With failure not an option, the company will draw up a cast-iron business plan and move ahead, making doubly sure of everything. But this approach usually ends in failure. I'd say the success rate is around 50 percent. Overly optimistic projections will come back to bite them. Unexpected developments will trip them up.

Investing is like gaining weight: The more you invest, the harder it becomes to move. You become unable to respond flexibly to change. It's better to be light and nimble on your feet when entering a new field, with its many uncertainties. Dinosaurs died out due to changes in the environment at the end of the Jurassic period. Our predecessors, who were able to survive this period, were small mammals not unlike the modern mouse.

Companies should continuously try new things, even if they're not major developments such as entering new fields. I call this the experimental phase. I think success depends on spending as little as possible during this phase, for the reasons I've already stated. It's better to be nimble. Cost reduction can also offer benefits. Cutting the amount spent in experimental phases increases the number of times you can afford to experiment. You can increase the number of business opportunities, rather than reducing them.

Of course, if you're confident you've achieved success in the experimental phase, you should sharply accelerate development. Success also depends on how fast you can do this. This is realized by keeping your organization lean. When the units in your organization are light and nimble and your structure is flexible, it won't take you long to scale the business, including appropriate allocation of people.

For companies, cost cutting is like the transformation of shedding skin. Just as caterpillars emerge from cocoons as butterflies, companies can evolve significantly via cost cutting.

The company with the largest cost advantage will always win.

80 Create *shikumi* that will keep generating value

There is a Japanese proverb that says tigers die and leave their skin, while people die and leave their names, but I have no interest in that kind of legacy. I want to leave behind *shikumi* that continually create new value.

The potential lifespan of a company is longer than a person's. At some point in the future, I will die and Rakuten will continue to exist. Rakuten as a company represents my ideals and so I want it to continue into the future. A company's essence is in its *shikumi*.

The cells that make up my body are continually being replaced, but I remain the same person. How can this be? Explaining this mysterious mechanism is a major topic of research in modern science.

Companies are similar in some ways. They can stay the same even if the people who make them up are replaced. However, in the case of a company, this mechanism is clear: It's the *shikumi*.

There are many *shikumi* within Rakuten: Some boost profits, some turn failures into successes, others are for team building, learning from other people, or developing employees. I believe the most important of these are the ones through which we continue to create value. In fact, we have many diverse *shikumi* that exist in order to continually drive value creation.

A company can't survive if it stops creating value.

Startups attract a lot of positive attention because they create new kinds of value. The attention doesn't last long, however, because new values age very quickly. I think the only way to continue to generate value is to consistently strive to enhance and improve every facet of what you do. There is no end to the process of improvement, or *kaizen*.

The biggest task I face in my work is the establishment of *shikumi* through which improvement can continue even after I'm gone. In that sense, even my goal of creating the best company in the world is also just a step toward achieving this.

As you build your company or advance your career, take time to consider: What *shikumi* will you pass on to others?

6

Nurture a Global Mindset

Y our business ideas change depending on how you view the world. To create new business models, you have to nurture a broad, realistic worldview.

81 The essence of e-commerce is communication

The internet is a tool that connects people. No matter how far technology advances, the essential qualities of people don't change. Human beings are living creatures who want to connect with others of their kind. The internet may have made countless things possible, but what hasn't changed is that fundamentally, it's a tool to connect people.

The Rakuten Ichiba shopping mall concept was born because we focused on this function: communication. People often stress the convenience and ease of purchasing things online, but these aren't the essential selling points. Rakuten Ichiba's defining feature is that it uses the internet to make a personal connection between shoppers and merchants: Its greatest strength is that it enables direct interaction with people all over Japan regardless of the location of physical stores.

There were already a few other internet shopping malls when I started Rakuten Ichiba. However, all of them basically employed a consignment sales model. The shopping mall handled everything from creating product catalogs and shipping products to dealing with customers.

I thought there was no way to succeed using this kind of system. Merchants know their products, better than anyone, and want to sell them more than anyone. Merchants ought to be far more passionate about creating catalogs and dealing with customers than any mall. For customers as well, dealing directly with the person responsible for a product is far more convenient. And above all, this arrangement helps foster communication between merchants and customers. Online shopping isn't just convenient, it's also fun. In fact, I'd go so far as to say it's more enjoyable than it is convenient. Online shopping is a form of entertainment.

That's why at Rakuten Ichiba, we had merchants create their own websites, ship their own products, and deal with their own customers. It's true that in the beginning, when many people knew nothing about the internet and had never touched a computer, many thought this would be impossible. Most believed creating websites and responding to customers' emails would be too difficult for people who weren't PC specialists.

However, if we'd done these things for merchants, we wouldn't have been able to leverage the fundamental merits of the internet. That's why we developed a system to enable even people who'd never touched a computer to create a simple website. Some may have struggled using the internet to interact with customers at first. But I believed communication with customers would go smoothly once sellers became more skilled PC users and that this would help them grow.

As a result, there are currently more than 44,000 sellers on Rakuten Ichiba. The secret to Rakuten's success is our sellers' highly attentive customer service. I would estimate there are at least 100,000 customer service specialists on the site. They support communication between stores and millions of customers every day. There are no shopping malls like this anywhere else in the world. Internet shops are not vending machines; the essence of e-commerce is communication.

82 Seek information beyond your borders

I don't mean to put down the Japanese media, but if you compare Japanese newspapers and magazines with European and US media you can't but help notice some fundamental differences.

For example, Japanese newspapers place a heavy emphasis on breaking news. It's critical for them to publish news stories ahead of rivals. It depends on the nature of the scoop, but I've hardly ever felt the value in doing this. My apologies to reporters who work hard to publish these scoops, but I wonder what's so great about reporting something half a day or a day earlier than the rest of the media. It has led to Japanese newspapers merely reporting bare facts, with very little room for editorial analysis.

Top European and US media are more focused on editorial analysis. Articles commonly include reporters' opinions and carry bylines. Media outlet rankings are determined by the quality of these opinions. Thus, quality media always carry outstanding editorials.

I always read the *Financial Times*. The opinions in its pages are in line with my thinking and are very useful when I'm mulling over different business directions. Of course, I also read Japan's leading business newspaper, the *Nikkei*, now the owner of the Financial Times. In fact, I don't feel quite right if I don't read it every morning. But I think in terms of the editorial content, it offers a different kind of reference point.

Of course, you should always closely follow local media, but I think everyone should also set time aside to read quality media sources from abroad. I recommend this to readers also as a way of boosting your capacity for logical thinking.

For Japanese people, being aware of world news can also be a kind of thought experiment. Things that happen elsewhere in the world won't necessarily happen in Japan. But thinking about what would happen in Japan if they did is a good way of practicing reading the future.

Despite globalization, there's still a time lag between when things happen elsewhere in the world and in Japan, and this will likely continue for a while. Aviation destroyed the barrier that was the Pacific Ocean, but the Japanese language barrier remains. Even the internet can't yet completely break down this barrier.

The global population is roughly 50 times the size of Japan's. By that rough calculation, 50 times as many things are happening outside Japan compared to inside it. Of course, news from around the world does make its way into Japan, but only a fraction.

When you start reading quality media sources from abroad, you might realize how unreliable your local media can be for knowing what's going on in the world.

When you open your eyes to the rest of the world, you realize how blinkered your view has been.

83 Your network is your best news source; media come second

In the previous section on global sources of information I recommended reading European and US newspapers. That said, always bear in mind that information that you acquire from newspapers, websites, television, or other forms of communication is already from a secondary source. This information can be accessed by anyone, and there's always a time lag between events and when you learn about them.

Strive to widen your sources of fresh, first-hand information.

If you're in the food industry, people working in agriculture, with livestock, or in fisheries can all be good sources of first-hand information. For those in web-based businesses, customers and end users are, of course, a good resource, as are university researchers and people in other retail businesses.

It's important to remember that information not directly relevant to your own business can also be valuable: Your view on the world will narrow considerably if you are constantly focused on your own work, and that alone.

While you can compensate for a narrow perspective with secondary sources such as various media outlets, that's simply not enough. To obtain fresh news, I recommend that you finish your work in good time every day and get out into the world. You can talk to your co-workers at work—so work on expanding your opportunities to hear the perspectives of people working in other industries.

In order to see modern civilization with their own eyes, the great figures of Japan's nineteenth century Meiji Restoration era undertook long and perilous journeys by sea to Europe and the United States, as this was their only choice for international travel at the time. The experiences they had and the emotions they felt drove Japan's modernization. As there were already many books and people from Europe and the United States in Japan at the time, it would have been possible to understand European and US culture through secondary sources like these. But of course, that wasn't enough.

Even when you have all the right information at your fingertips, there are simply many things that, when experienced directly, create a completely different impression. Information from a secondary source has already passed through someone else's brain and, in the process, their subjective choices and viewpoints have entered the equation.

You can't accurately understand current trends through secondary sources alone.

Of course, you can't directly confirm with your own eyes and ears all of the huge number of sources of information in today's world. Realistically, no matter how often you go out into the world, you'll still be forced to rely mostly on secondary sources for your information. However, whether or not you make an effort to obtain first-hand information will also make a big difference to how effectively you use that second-hand information as well. For example, when you hear news about New York, the depth of your understanding will be different depending on whether you've actually walked its streets and breathed its air—be it only once. If you make friends with someone you can trust in New York, you'll be able to analyze the news from yet another angle.

The further the Internet Age progresses, the more valuable information that is experienced directly is likely to become. To grasp trends ahead of anyone else, strive to increase the amount of first-hand information you receive via your personal and professional network.

Create your own independent information network to stay abreast of the trends of the day.

84 The internet will eliminate national borders. Think global

I've already written about my belief that the internet will bring about a kind of worldwide revolution, transforming the way we think about nations and borders. To prepare for this, you must first eliminate the borders within your own mind.

For a long time, Japan had two barriers, namely its language and the ocean, isolating it from the rest of the world. You might say Japan was protected from the waves of turmoil arising overseas. That Japan developed a unique culture and civilization in this sheltered world is something to be proud of.

However, Japan failed to develop mature skills for interacting with the rest of the world in this period and still seems to be feeling the aftereffects of this, even in the twenty-first century.

For many Japanese people, "the world" is still a different planet you visit for a time and then return from. It's as if Japan is different, and not really part of the world. Thus, no matter where we go, many Japanese people always feel like "guests" in someone else's world. We find it difficult to really feel that Japan is a part of the world, fully connected to it—even though we understand the concept. That's why news from abroad can feel like news about someone else's world that is not particularly relevant. If a problem arises in the Middle East, even one with a clear and direct impact on Japan, most people will think it doesn't concern them.

In contrast, and this is just my subjective view, it seems to me that the attention Westerners pay to news from overseas is about the same that Japanese people give to news from other regions of Japan.

In business, Europeans and Americans target foreign markets as a matter of course, while Japanese businesspeople, in spite of the interconnectedness between the Japanese and world economies, still talk about "advancing into the world" as though it is something unusual or special.

We should consciously strive to change this way of thinking.

It's easy to say that we're all part of the same world. But for the average Japanese person on the street, it's difficult to really feel that in their heart. If we don't change this attitude, we won't be able to adapt when the internet really does do away with the concept of national borders. We'll be at the mercy of waves of people, capital, and information flowing into Japan, and we'll lose sight of the path our nation should follow.

85 Learn from the world's best practices

Just as people don't often notice examples of success that are close to home, they also have a blind spot for another kind of success—that of the very best in the world. Think about them: Why are they so successful? Can you put the reason into words? People tend not to think too deeply about what seems obvious. It's a flaw of the human psyche.

Einstein reportedly once remarked how strange he found it that clouds float in the sky. He noted most adults didn't think it was odd, but that he still did even as an adult because he was a late bloomer. He said it was the reason he became a scientist.

The same is true of business.

Just as there's a reason why clouds float in the sky, there's also a reason why the world's "best" have achieved that position. So you should analyze those reasons and apply what you learn to your own business.

You'll immediately understand this if you spend some time looking into it, but the companies that become the best in the world all have something unique. Industry leaders differ substantially from typical companies in their sectors. A normal company will never constitute a standout example of success.

This might surprise you at first, but give it some thought and you'll realize it's obvious: You can't reach the top using established methods. It's when you succeed at something no one else has ever thought of that you can escape from being average. Thus, the world's top companies are all unique. However, for some reason, their true uniqueness often goes unnoticed. It seems people become so dazzled by their business performance that they mistake uniqueness for "special circumstances" as the reason behind that success. Actually, those "special circumstances" are what's masking the reason for that company's success. Of course, it won't be easy to apply those secrets directly to your own business. If it were easy, other companies would already be doing it.

However, when you get past those special circumstances and find the fundamental reasons why leading companies do so well, you can leverage them in your own business.

Extract the essence of the uniqueness of the world's top companies and distill it to universal principles that can be applied in other fields. Think like Einstein—study the world's best practices and master the fundamental principles of success.

And never forget how strange it is that clouds float in the sky.

86 Thinking globally will make you stronger locally

If you only ever look at your own country, you will lose the ability to clearly see what's in front of you. It's only when you go abroad that you see your country's true face for the first time. Through comparison with something else, you are able to see more clearly your own characteristics and unique points.

In this context, thinking globally also means looking in from the outside. In short, thinking globally will help make your own country even better. I really felt this strongly when Japan's economic bubble burst at the beginning of the 1990s.

I realized why Japan's financial institutions were at a disadvantage. For people in Japan, the bursting of the economic bubble was unprecedented. Land and share prices plummeted, and there were fears the economy might fall into an abyss. These fears led to assets being sold at rock-bottom prices. Overseas financial institutions jumped in and bought up the property at rock-bottom prices. Buying in at the bottom of the market is a strength of global financial institutions because they operate with a global perspective.

However, if you understood the global context, you could see that the bubble was clearly just a phase. Even land prices are cyclical. Prices are always low at some point, and if you buy at these times you'll be sure to make a profit. Investors judged the situation based on their experiences around the world and reaped huge profits. This global mindset transformed the bursting of Japan's economic bubble into a business opportunity.

The strength of global companies is their ability to identify successful models in markets around the world and apply them in other markets.

Japan is currently struggling with various domestic issues that could probably be addressed with solutions from new perspectives if we could just stop focusing only on Japan and look at things from a global viewpoint. I'm not suggesting that we examine examples from abroad and draw up a bunch of empty theories. It's not about glancing next door, seeing how they do something and thinking you might try it yourself. What I'm talking about is engaging fully with the world and planting firm roots in it. When I approached this issue, I realized that in order to understand and learn from the innovation culture of Silicon Valley, I would need roots there. Not just a trip or a research project, but time on the ground. It's a core reason I founded Crimson House West, our San Mateo headquarters for the Americas. Some months, I spend as much as half my time in that office.

You mustn't view what happens abroad as something that doesn't concern you. As someone living in the same world, make it your business to understand what other countries are really like, then look again at Japan from a new perspective. That is what it takes to think globally.

87 Thoroughly and humbly analyze past successes

Human beings like to show off. Although there are many reasons we want to succeed, attention-seeking is one that must not be overlooked. I think this desire might not be limited to humans. Even cats like to show off the animals they catch to their owners. We all want to be recognized for how special we are: It's a deeply rooted desire in us all.

We often try and do things our own way because we want to show off, we want to prove that our way is the right way. And we usually fail.

Modern humans are conceited in another way, too: We think we're living in the most advanced civilization ever. We think we're marching toward the future and that stale history books have nothing to teach us. But I believe we should put more thought into it than this.

True, a hundred years ago there were no computers. But does that make modern people who use computers great? How many people know what's inside their PC? Never mind PCs—if you asked people to make a mobile phone, a TV, or even a match, how many could do it?

The advanced civilization we enjoy just happens to be part of the world we were born into. We take advantage of it, with no real understanding of its frameworks or structures. Moreover, the things we do with it are just a virtual repeat of the things people did long ago.

For example, Edo (as Tokyo was once called), with a population of around one million, had virtually all the amenities of similar size towns today. If you look it up, you might be surprised. Edo had a media industry, a recycling industry, restaurants, of course, and even temp agencies.

Organizations go through the same development processes in every age, and the reasons organizations succeed or fail are also broadly similar. There are many commonalities to be found among the problems and pitfalls they face on the way up, and the reasons why they decline.

Civilizations change, but perhaps human beings don't.

Just by looking at recent history (you don't have to go as far back as the Edo Period), you'll find plenty of hints as to how to overcome the barriers you face today. Viewed this way, human history is like a valuable collection of the results of countless trial-and-error experiments. We must put this to good use.

Throw away your conceit and your meaningless need for attention. In the end, those who ultimately succeed are those who study with humility. This is another thing that history has taught me.

88 It's never too late

There's a term called *first-mover advantage*. The first person to take action has a natural advantage.

And it's certainly true. Being the first to act is a great advantage, especially out on the business frontier of the internet. When you go into uncharted territory, where no competitor precedes you, you're free to take up as much land as you like.

Those who come later are robbed of this advantage. Because competition is fierce, they have to work hard to survive. They can't capture as much of the territory as those who came first. So first-mover advantage is about the importance of being the first person to go into frontier territory.

That said, it's also never too late to start something. If you start now, you can do anything. I truly believe this.

True, coming late to the game puts you at a disadvantage, and winning won't be easy—as anyone will tell you. Don't expect an easy win. But if you plot out your grand strategy and are prepared to invest the time, you can turn just about any situation around.

This is where sports differ from business. In soccer, you must win within 90 minutes. In business, you decide your own time limits. If winning in 90 minutes is impossible, you can do it in 10 years.

Rakuten Ichiba was not the first mover. We came into the market when everyone thought the internet shopping mall model was a thing of the past. But despite that, we have come a long way. I learned that just because someone else has moved first, it does not mean all the moves have been made. There may still be moves yet untried—moves the first player failed to consider.

Even now, as we begin to expand abroad, we face a situation in which many countries already have services similar to our own. Many say we won't succeed, but I completely disagree.

Just as there's the phrase *first-mover advantage*, we could also talk about a *best-mover advantage*. It means those who act in the best way have an advantage. Just because others acted first, that doesn't mean they acted best. And even if their ways were best initially, it doesn't mean that there aren't better ways to do things now.

If you're not the first mover, be the best mover.

In life, it's never too late.

Acknowledgments

Many people contributed to the creation of this book and, in line with the lessons in the book, I would like to thank as many of them as I can here. My apologies for not being able to name everyone here in the text but the teams at Rakuten in the CEO Office and Corporate Communications moved mountains, large and small, to make sure this book reached completion.

Leah Spiro of Riverside Creative Management both championed the book and kept a keen eye out for relevance for the non-Japanese reader. Bill Falloon at Wiley guided the project with his characteristic passion for management principles from different cultural perspectives. Ellen Neuborne has been a great supporter on editing, bringing a fresh and thorough eye to the text that we translated, largely internally, from the Japanese original. On translation, the internal team made a terrific effort, as well as making the most of the wise insights of Adam Fulford and his team.

Of course, without the publication of the original Japanese book, "Golden Rules of Success", with the warm support and understanding of the team at Gentosha, this project would not have been possible.

And without the inspiration of all the people I have worked with over the years, at Rakuten and at companies and organizations both inside and outside Japan, as well as the discipline of organizing my thoughts every week for all the employees at our internal all-hands Asakai meetings, and the intelligent and honest feedback of my life partner, Haruko, I would not have been ready to write this book. I thank each one of you for what has been an amazing journey and I am looking forward to continuing to learn from you.

Index